libro
Grueso

THE
Everlasting South

"The Everlasting South"

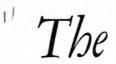

FRANCIS BUTLER SIMKINS

LOUISIANA STATE UNIVERSITY PRESS

TO

JOHN E. TALMADGE

a son of the unchanging South

FOREWORD

For more than three decades Professor Francis Butler Simkins has studied and taught the history of the South. His books and essays have enriched the literature on the region. His scalpel book reviews have dissected scores of writings about the South, and have cleanly parted sound scholarship and exposition from superficiality and jargon. His lectures—whether formal in the classroom or casual "under the campus oaks"—have kindled the minds of thousands of students. The keenness of his intellect, the warmth of his friendship, the courtliness of his address, and the innumerable striking eccentricities of his manner have united to endear him to a host of associates and admirers. Professor Simkins is a personage among Southern historians.

Professor Simkins is a native of South Carolina. He received the Ph.D. degree from Columbia University in 1926. He has taught at many Southern colleges and universities, including Randolph-Macon Woman's College, Emory University, Louisiana State University, and Longwood College in

Farmville, Virginia, where he is now Professor of History. He has been a visiting professor at the University of North Carolina, the University of Texas, and Princeton University. In 1932 Professor Simkins received the Dunning Prize of the American Historical Association. He has held research fellowships of the Social Science Research Council and the John Simon Guggenheim Memorial Foundation. He once delivered the Walter Lynwood Fleming Lectures in Southern History at Louisiana State University. In 1954 Professor Simkins was president of the Southern Historical Association.

No single label will adequately describe Professor Simkins' scholarship. At a time when most students of Southern history still looked upon Reconstruction as the "chamber of horrors" in the region's past, he took a leading role in proclaiming the Revisionist school of thought. The travail and racial strife of Reconstruction have been exaggerated in Southern folklore and in scholarly writings alike, he said: actually, life in those times was reasonably satisfying; and the Carpetbagger-Scalawag-Negro constitutional conventions and legislatures attempted many beneficial and lasting reforms for the South. Professor Simkins' *South Carolina During Reconstruction* (Chapel Hill, 1932), written in collaboration with Robert H. Woody, trended to such a conclusion; Professor Simkins' "New Viewpoints of Southern Reconstruction" called for a fresh appraisal of the epoch along this line.

Professor Simkins' *Pitchfork Ben Tillman, South Carolinian* (Baton Rouge, 1944) is a sympathetic yet candid biography of the great South Carolina demagogue.

But Professor Simkins' most persistent theme has been that a distinctive South really does exist; that it has a mind and culture of its own; that—to paraphrase Wilbur Cash—

the South is not quite a nation within a nation, but that it is almost one. Professor Simkins sees the South as a unique blend of race and family consciousness, personal violence, protestant orthodoxy, political conservatism, and economic colonialism; of total abstinence surrounded by tippling; of literary genius in the midst of intellectual indifference and nonliteracy; of implacable sectional loyalty entwined with national chauvinism; and of drawling speech, feminine women, and hot biscuits. The theme of the enduring South pervades his general history of the South, *The South Old and New: A History 1820–1947* (New York, 1947), and its revised and expanded edition, *A History of the South* (New York, 1963). This is the theme of four of Professor Simkins' essays appearing in the present volume.

In the discourse, "Tolerating the South's Past," Professor Simkins scores the tendency of modern historians to judge Southern institutions of old by the standards of today. Let the region's historians follow the practice of the great twentieth-century Southern novelists, urges Professor Simkins; let the historians write a "literature of accommodation" instead of a literature of censure. In "The South's Democratic Pose," Professor Simkins argues that, at the core, Southern ideals are aristocratic and not democratic, as the South pretends them to be. The region would be more dignified, he says, if it would shed its pretenses, and proclaim forthright its belief in distinctions of race and class.

In "The Rising Tide of Faith," Professor Simkins considers Southern religion as a binding element in the homogeneity of the Southern people. The "Solid South" is more solid in faith, he reasons, than in politics. Moreover, since the churches are presumably beyond government coercion, Professor Simkins predicts that Southern religion will continue indefinitely to conserve the regional identity. "The South as a Region" is a sweeping reaffirmation of Professor Simkins' belief in the South's ability to adjust to national demands but still retain the Southern ethos.

Probably a great majority of historians today disagree with Professor Simkins' logic in the last four of these discourses. But probably a great majority of the common folk of the South, wittingly or unwittingly, agree with the gist of it. If so, the very presence of such a body of opinion would seem to support Professor Simkins' claim that a distinctive South really does exist. Accept his reasoning or reject it, these essays express the central theme of one of the South's most brilliant scholars.

CHARLES P. ROLAND
Professor of History
Tulane University

PREFACE

THE region below the Potomac, judging from the titles of books by recent scholars and journalists, is becoming very different from what it once was. *The Changing South, The Advancing South, Requiem for Dixie, The Emerging South*—implicit in these is the assertion that the region is now approximating the national ideal of progress and democracy. Gunnar Myrdal in *An American Dilemma* implies that the South is uneasy because it violates the American creed of equality in regard to the Negro.

The authors of these books attempt to prove that the South is retreating from its old ways before the forces of progressive nationalism. As evidence they cite the fact that the region has almost unanimously adopted the ideals and practices of Northern industrialism, that machinery in Southern mills is as modern as its Northern counterpart, that the new business of the South, supervised by the overseers of Northern capital, is as much admired by the common people as were the plantations and planters of the Old South, that machines imported from the North have in many instances bulldozed the Southern landscape out of its original contours, that universal education of the Massachusetts and Ohio variety is so graciously received by all classes of Southern people that compulsory education laws are scarcely necessary.

The attempt of the United States Supreme Court in 1954 to break the South's seemingly immutable custom of separating the races in schools was resisted by many devices. But the resort to violence, an effective tactic during Reconstruction, was frustrated by the descent of the "Assyrian host" in the form of Federal troops upon communities which disobeyed decrees of the Federal courts. Legal actions against these decrees met in almost all cases with adverse judicial action.

Nevertheless, there is no reason to discard Stark Young's contention that "the changing South is still the South." Indeed it can be argued that the region, despite many changes, is as much different from the rest of the United States today as it was in 1860. The Old South, until the firing of the first guns of the Civil War, was as fervently patriotic to the Union as was the New South at the time of World War I. Both the Old and the New South were Anglo-Saxon, nativist, and Protestant, and both were as much inclined before the Civil War as since to meet in battle the enemies of the United States. Bloodshed in 1861 was the case of brother meeting brother in combat; land-hungry Southerners fighting land-hungry Northerners; Bible-reading Anglo-Saxons fighting Bible-reading Anglo-Saxons. One of the reasons the South lost the war was that its desire to separate from the rest of the country was not sufficiently developed.

In a sense the Confederate States of America was not born until after it was dead. Ironically it was not until after the Conquered Banner had been folded, when Reconstruction decrees attempted to make the Negro equal to the Caucasian, that the South became fully conscious of its distinction from other parts of the United States.

The South since 1865 has failed to attract many immigrants. The growing cities of the New South, enveloped in the rural psychology that surrounds them, have little of the cosmopolitanism that blew from Europe into Northern cities. The South became increasingly religious while the North grew more skeptical and worldly.

In the middle of the twentieth century, the North attempted to impose its concept of race upon the supposedly backward South; this endeavor resulted in many constitutional, moral, and intellectual conquests for the majority section. Nevertheless, the South won many emotional and psychological victories. When the North tried to impose Reconstruction a second time, it found the average white Southerner viewing the venture as a more serious threat to his philosophy of living than was the first Reconstruction in the 1870's.

The first of these five essays is an attempt to apply an element of sound historical scholarship. Take pride, I contend, in the South as it is today without assuming that the land of slavery and nullification had no justification for existence. Historians apply this criterion to the Middle Ages. Why not apply it to the Old South?

This article is followed by an essay which demonstrates that the South's adherence to the national creed of equality of all men is belied by a multitude of social distinctions aside from racial prejudice. In the South the various classes of white people do not mix in intimate social contact; persons who are socially or economically inferior know their place and must act accordingly.

Another essay recognizes ways in which the South is different in important respects from the rest of the country. These differences should be tolerated to prove the existence of a Southern region and contradict Sinclair Lewis' idea that the United States is a vast series of main streets.

"New Viewpoints of Southern Reconstruction" shows that the sequel to Appomattox was far milder than Southern legend contends. Nevertheless, that period is still regarded by most white Southerners as the most horrible of their experiences, because efforts were made to take Negroes out of the groove in which Southern custom had placed them.

The final essay demonstrates that the "old-time religion," with impressive modern variations, has taken hold of the region with an intensity that makes its importance second only to racial attitudes. Christian orthodoxy is stronger in the South than in any other section of the United States.

Americanism, as Southerners know it, extends to the desire to fight passionately for the United States when it is assailed by a foreign foe. But the region retains its desire to be different in such important matters as race attitudes and religion. Despite the protests of nationalistic politicians and scholars wedded to concepts of national progress, the thesis of this book is that the South has been successful in maintaining these differences.

The author and LSU Press are grateful to the following publishers for permission to reprint these articles: "Tolerating the South's Past," the *Journal of Southern History;* "The South's Democratic Pose," *The Georgia Review;* "The South as a Region," Merrill Jensen (ed.), *Regionalism in America* (University of Wisconsin Press, 1951); "New Viewpoints of Southern Reconstruction," the *Journal of Southern History;* and "The Rising Tide of Faith," Louis D. Rubin, Jr. and James J. Kilpatrick (eds.), *The Lasting South* (Chicago, 1957).

F.B.S.

Farmville, Virginia
April, 1963

CONTENTS

THE
Everlasting South

ONE

TOLERATING THE SOUTH'S PAST

THE AGE of Enlightenment represented the Middle Ages as a Gothic night—an interlude of ignorance and superstition when men were enveloped in a cowl, oblivious to the wonders of knowledge, and concerned only with escape from the miseries of this world and of hell. Voltaire said that Dante was considered a great poet because no one read him, that a Gothic cathedral was a monument to the stupidity of its builders. The humility of holy men and the faith of the Catholic offended the egotism, skepticism, and common sense of the leaders of the Enlightenment.

Historians of the nineteenth and twentieth centuries have thrown aside the conceits of those who went before them and have learned to appraise the medieval age in terms of its own values. It is now recognized as a period when the Christian church and an imaginative architecture flowered, when artists were humble enough to glorify God rather than themselves, and when universities, chivalry, and vernacular literatures had their beginnings.

The reputation of the region of the United States below the Potomac today suffers from the same forces from which the Middle Ages suffered at the hands of historians during the Enlightenment. Chroniclers of Southern history often do not grasp the most elementary concept of sound historiography: the ability to appraise the past by standards other than those of the present. They accept a fanatical nationalism which leaves little room for sectional variations, a faith in Darwinian progress which leaves no room for static contentment, and a faith in the American dream of human equality which leaves little room for one person to get ahead of another except in making money. In theory at least, our historians refuse to tolerate the concept of "all sorts and conditions of men" of which *The Book of Common Prayer* speaks.

Growing out of the uncritical acceptance by historians of the South of this creed of contemporary Americans are certain concrete dogmas: the church and the state should be separate, but not the school and the state; school but not church attendance should be compulsory; universal education is better than folk culture; political democracy is better than aristocratic rule; freedom is better than slavery; nationalism is better than provincialism; urban standards are better than rural ones; small farms are better than plantations; the larger the number of voters the better the commonwealth; and the two-party system is better than the harmony of one party.

I am not asking the abandonment of any of these dogmas as bases for action in the world of today. They constitute the American Dream on which much prosperity and hope is built. I am asking that Southern historians not hide this fact: our ancestors did not hold to these dogmas in every situation of life, and especially in those aspects of their lives which explain their regionalism. I am also asking Southern historians not to accuse their ancestors of being stupid or unreasonable in this respect.

The historians who are friendly to the region and who accept the ideal of human equality seem ashamed of the degree to which the South has not attained this ideal. In defense of their beloved region, the hopeful among them find evidences of the struggle of the lower classes for a greater degree of equality. They present the followers of Nathaniel Bacon as yeomen farmers rebelling against a planter dictatorship. They give credence to many rumors of slave insurrections, and they often envisage the common people rising against political oligarchies. Their faith in the benefits of two political parties has led them to predict, for the past ten decades, the breakup of the solid South and the coming of a state of rectitude like that of New York or Illinois. They are apologetic over the existence in the South of the sharpest social distinction in all America: that between the white man and the Negro. They hail breaks in the color line as forecasts of the good times a-coming.

Their attitude, when proclaimed by publicists and politicians, may be justified as accommodation to the dominant ideals of the ruling part of the United States. But such diplomacy applied to issues of the past convicts historians of naïveté or what the French and the Germans call Anglo-Saxon hypocrisy.

Those who accept national unity as the ultimate goal of all Americans find it difficult to defend a region whose chief distinction is that it attempted to destroy that unity. The friendly historian often chooses States' Rights or secession as his theme. He emphasizes the existence of minorities who adhered to the national rather than the sectional cause. He gives honor to such nationalists as Andrew Jackson and Andrew Johnson instead of to such divisionists as John Randolph and John C. Calhoun. He seems almost to get his inspiration from William T. Sherman who felt justified in imposing a cruel punishment upon the South because it tried to destroy the national unity.

Why do not our historians take their cue from Sinclair Lewis when he condemns America to an esthetic hell because most of its regions have succeeded in ironing out their provincial differences? Why are they not proud of the fact that Lewis' criticisms apply least of all to the South? If this were not true, the South would not be worth writing about. Let historians take for themselves the task of understanding and appreciating the sectional variations.

There is a reality about the South which historians with egalitarian standards find hard to comprehend. This reality is that many of the so-called advances in equality turn out to be imaginary. Freedom, for example, to the early Georgians meant revolt against the tyranny of foreign despots. Georgians did not want to be saved from the social and economic inequalities of the other Southern colonies through prohibition of slavery and large estates. The so-called rising of the Virginians in the American Revolution against oppressors turns out to be, in the light of modern researches, the struggle of an aggressive aristocracy against an official oligarchy, with the common man following noisily the leadership of his social betters. There is much that is artificial and sentimental in Virginia's greatest political philosopher advocating the equality of man and at the same time owning slaves, living in a house which Europeans would call a palace, and tolerating a political machine as oligarchical as that of Harry F. Byrd. A paradox of Southern history is that progress in political

democracy was often followed by the desire of the newly enfranchised to destroy certain aspects of equality. The freer
exercise of the suffrage by the common white man in the
1890's was followed by the Jim Crow laws and the disfranchisement of most of the Negroes. Those who got the vote
under the Jacksonian reforms of the 1830's were pleased when
their leader was transformed into a planter and a Southern
gentleman; and when a catty journalist accused Rachel Jackson of smoking a pipe, there was resentment among the descendants of the original Jacksonians. Earlier, the Jacksonian
reforms had been followed by the strengthening of the slave
code and the disfranchisement of the free persons of color.

The Southern Negro has never got much beyond federal
ukase in his enthusiasm for closing the social gap separating
him from Southern whites. As a slave, he never carried out a
general rising against his masters. The equalities which after
the Civil War were supposed to be his never got beyond a narrow political stage: the Negro never until recently made a
determined demand for social equality. In withdrawing from
the white churches he surrendered an element of social in-
timacy with the white man which he had experienced under
slavery. In our day he has been invited to attend white
churches, but in many cases he does not want to accept this
invitation. The most exalted outside interventionists in the
social arrangements of the South recently restored suffrage
to the Negro, but he turned around and joined the political
party of the white oligarchy.

Much is written by our historians concerning the Negro's
discontent with his caste status and the progress he has made
in changing this status. There is some reality in these assertions, but many times it is forgotten that the white man has
more often been discontented with the Negro than the Negro

with the white man. Those of us who, through the years, have known Southern life intimately, are familiar with the constant complaints leveled against the exasperating race. The white man has been able to act on his complaints as effectively as the Negro has on his. In recent decades the white man, for example, sharpened the color line and took business and residential opportunities away from the black man.

It is time that historians who explain or defend the South recognize the existence of social hierarchy. They can be sympathetic toward it without being illogical, remembering that arguments advanced for social gradations by Plato are as logical as arguments advanced to the contrary. They should realize that the arguments of Jefferson Davis and James D. B. De Bow in favor of the gradations in slave society had more influence on the nonslaveholding whites than did the arguments advanced by Hinton R. Helper and other enemies of Southern social practices. They should know that the color line was created to sustain the most important fact in Southern history. Two biologically aggressive races have dwelt together in large numbers for 340 years without the ruling race losing its integrity of blood. Without this fact there would be no South in the social or psychological sense; the region between the Potomac and the Rio Grande would be just a geographical expression.

The historian of the South should accept the class and race distinctions of his region unless he wishes to deplore the region's existence. He should display a tolerant understanding of why the Goddess of Justice has not always been blind in the South, why there have been lynchings and Jim Crow laws, why the legend of the Cavaliers exists, and why, as William Alexander Percy puts it, "Even today from Virginia to Texas ten thousand crepuscular old maids in ghostly coveys and clusters" seek to trace their ancestors. Our historian should stop trying to prove that the maidens of the Old South did not always have wasp waists and stand on colonnaded porches attended by bandannaed mammies who did not have wasp waists. At least one Southern historian, Francis P. Gaines, has retired from the iconoclastic task of trying to prove that the Old South was not what it is supposed to have been. He became the keeper of the tomb of the knight whom not even our most energetic fact-finder has accused of being unworthy of the company of King Arthur.

A logical consequence of the disparagement of the sectional values is that the leader who tried hardest to break the national unity has fared badly at the hands of his biographers. They condemn Jefferson Davis as a prolonged conspirator against the Union. But the facts show that as late as 1860 he, as a United States senator, was advocating appropriations for the army he was to fight in less than a year. A proper sympathy for the sectional values would perhaps lead to a condemnation of Davis because he did not become a conspirator against the Union soon enough. Unlike Caesar or Hitler, Davis was not one of the great revolutionists of history; he was too honorable for that. Unlike William L. Yancey and R. Barnwell Rhett, he was slow in understanding that the North was in a revolutionary conspiracy against the Constitution as he interpreted it, a conspiracy which could be answered effectively only by counterrevolution. The poet Allen Tate is the only biographer who condemns Davis for not understanding that the aim of the plutocratic democracy of the North was to crush his beloved Southland.

Davis should be praised for at last recognizing the forces arrayed against his section and then heroically defending its concept of truth and justice. Despite physical weaknesses, he maintained a proud but ragged nation for four years against the powers of wealth, progress, and patriotism. After defeat he did not repent.

For his failure to repent, historians do not forgive Davis. He did not respond to the new wave of nationalism which came after the Civil War. He was no pragmatist, no evolutionist. Until his death he remained in spirit the slavemaster, the soldier who found greatest virtue in continuing the battle charge after the enemy had inflicted a grievous wound, and remained the scholastic who accepted the Bible and the Constitution just as they were written. He was as optimistic in his devotion to the antique values of the South as was Don Quixote to the antique values of an older land. If the historians of the South were as tolerant of our past as are the European historians of theirs, they would confer on the defeated President of the Confederacy as many honors as have been conferred on the Spanish knight.

Friendly Southern historians bolster the pride of the section by exaggerating the ways in which the South approximated the achievements of the North. Ignoring the Negro third of the population, they emphasize the degree to which the Old South achieved political democracy and universal education. Remembering prejudices against the large landowner, they emphasize the role of the yeoman farmer in Southern agriculture. Ignoring the prejudices of the people against foreigners, they make much of isolated cases of foreigners who found the South congenial. And, in refutation of the assertion that the region has been a Sahara of talent, long lists have been compiled of Southerners who played eminent roles in the building of the nation.

The candid observer must admit that, according to the urban standards of the North and of Europe, Frederick Law

Olmsted's harsh judgment on the paucity of Southern culture has remained sound for most of the hundred years since this nosy New Englander wrote. Perhaps the reason the *Dictionary of American Biography* has articles on only 724 natives of Virginia compared with articles on 1,763 natives of Massachusetts is that Southerners have been indifferent to those in their midst who have had latent talents in music, sculpture, painting, and the other arts. In the South Carolina of my youth the only art we recognized was English and Northern literature. We read Walter Scott and James Fenimore Cooper; we did not read William Gilmore Simms. We recognized native greatness only in war and in politics.

It is true that in recent years the South has learned to acclaim native eminence in literature and in business. But a Southern book to be acceptable to Southerners must first hit the New York sounding board. Our distinguished businessmen are often dependent on Wall Street to promote and finance the South's industrial expansion. For mechanical inventions, the most creative of American achievements, the South has been dependent upon the North. Its people do not invent or manufacture the machinery of its industry: it is still as colonial as Asia or South America in this respect.

Our historians should explain or justify these supposed deficiencies of the South by showing that its genius is rural, not urban; that the larger the cities grow the more countrified they become because of the rural origin of their newer inhabitants. Our historians should also explain that our townsmen build country-style houses, that they have little or nothing to contribute to the urban amenities, and that they support comparatively few good restaurants, theaters, orchestras, or book stores. As in the days of the English traveler George W. Featherstonhaugh, they talk of hogs, horses, and

cows when they are not talking about the mechanical con-
trivances Northerners have sold them.

The true Southerner should take pride that the South's
fame is based on tobacco, hogs, rice, and cotton, and that its
greatest man is the country gentleman with his cult of hospitality, his sense of leisure, his neglect of the passion for
trade, his capacity to refurbish old mansions and to build new
ones in imitation of the old, and his creative interest in the
rehabilitation of antique furniture. In his capacity as a farmer
the Southern gentleman has been creative from the days of
John Rolfe and George Washington down to the day of our
professors of agriculture and of our merchant-farmers. Our
professors of agriculture perfect new seeds and varieties of
animals; our merchant-farmers establish farms with green
pastures which serve as models for professional farmers. If
the South has had an internal revolution since 1865, it is the
type of endeavor in which the people have adhered most
firmly to the traditions of their ancestors. The revolution has
been in agriculture.

Southern historians, trapped by the belief that education is
a cure-all, have exaggerated the accomplishments of formal
schooling. They like to prove that Sir William Berkeley was
inaccurate when he said that there were no free schools in
seventeenth-century Virginia. They are dazzled that today
we have "a triumphant 'progressive' education which progresses even faster than the North." They gloss over the defects of our much-praised educational system. They should remember that our public schools have affronted the American
dogma of the universality of education, treating the Negroes
differently from other people and at one time prohibiting
them from going to school. They should realize that we of
the South indulged to a greater degree than other people in

"the education that does not educate" in the sense of changing people, presumedly for the better, in the arts of living and in outlook on life.

Historians would be wise to admit the defects of Southern education as measured by the proclaimed goals of American public schools; indeed they might be skeptical of these goals. They might admit that Berkeley was not a complete fool when he inveighed against schools and presses. The defender of this seventeenth-century gentleman can find comfort in high scholarly authority of the twentieth century. Arnold J. Toynbee wrote in 1947: "The bread of universal education is no sooner cast upon the water than a shoal of sharks [the presslords] arises from the depths and devours the children's bread under the educator's very eyes." Southern historians should realize that the faith in the rule of the educated common man has brought us no nearer the millennium than were our ancestors in the eighteenth century.

Historians of the South agree with Montesquieu that a political structure should "fit the humor and disposition of the people," and yet they judge the educational achievements of a rural people by standards imported from Prussia by way of New England. This Prussian-type school was loaded with antislavery sentiments and with notions of social reform repulsive to a region of Christians not dominated by hopes of earthly perfection. The leveling tendencies of the new schools ran counter to the Old South's conception of hierarchy. Their content was more suited for those who needed guidance for town life than for a people whose chief task was to subdue a wilderness and to establish farms.

Someone should tell that the South's resistance to formal schooling did not grow out of laziness or stupidity. This resistance was a vital part of the region's attempt to survive as a social and cultural entity. The South unconsciously fought against the idea that the school be allowed to iron out provincial differences in order to make the Southern states into undifferentiated units of the republic. Southerners have preserved their folkways and ancestral superstitions, thereby avoiding the fate of the people of Hawaii, a people who have deliberately escaped their ancestral heritage in order to be Americanized through the public schools.

Our chroniclers should quit being ashamed of the cloud of illiteracy which once hung over their province. They should wake up to the fact that the unschooled Uncle Remus was among the wisest Southerners. They have stressed the benefits of the schools to such a degree that they have neglected the triumphs of informal training outside the school. This informal education was good because it was useful. Our colonial and frontier ancestors put the arts of subduing the wilderness first; they learned to use the ax and the rifle extremely well. With some justice they regarded formal education as an adornment of the upper classes.

The dark spot on Southern civilization of denying formal education to the slaves can be wiped out by an understanding of what was accomplished in the so-called school of the plantation in which the barbarian captive from Africa was Anglicized. This was a type of training more effective than anything the South has experienced since. The slave was so well inoculated with Anglo-American culture that almost all elements of his African background disappeared. The Negro imbibed the rich heritage of European folklore and became so skilled in English handicrafts and in the intricate practices of plantation agriculture that he was perhaps better educated in the industrial arts than those Negroes who have lived since the time of Booker T. Washington.

The acceptance by our historians of the national faith in equality has led them to neglect the constructive role of class distinctions and aristocracy in Southern culture. The masses of the South imitate the upper classes with so much enthusiasm that most of the section's approved practices and attitudes are of upper-class origin. I can think of only two popular social diversions of lower-class origin: jazz music and corn whisky. The aristocratic pretensions of all classes are so strong that everybody thinks of himself as a gentleman. Wilbur J. Cash observes that the yeoman farmers of the Old South adopted from the plantation aristocracy "a kindly courtesy, a level-eyed pride, an easy quietness, a barely perceptible flourish of bearing, which for all its obvious angularity and fundamental plainness was one of the finest things the Old South produced." And the Jeeter Lesters, for all their ignorance and barbarism, possessed aristocratic attitudes, hating manual toil and taking on, as Cash says, "a sort of unkempt politeness and ease of port, which rendered them definitely superior to their peers in the rest of the country."

A majority of Southerners believes that the nearest approach to heaven this side of the grave is that aristocratic perfection known as the Old South. This was not only the belief of Walter Hines Page's "mummies," but also of such innovators as Daniel A. Tompkins, Ben Tillman, and Tom Watson. One finds it in the writings of such divergent persons as Thomas Nelson Page and William Faulkner. Then it was, so runs the legend of the Old South, that the Virginia gentleman lived in a feudal splendor that was justified by the belief that he had ancestors from the novels of Walter Scott; that the Mississippi gentleman's comparable splendors were justified by the belief that he had Virginia ancestors. These beliefs are supplemented by the assertion that the Confederate soldier because he was always brave was also always virtuous. The fact that all classes in the South cherish the aristocratic concept has brought about a unity of spirit which results in a friendly tie between the masses and the classes.

A host of Southern historians would prove, through the collection of multitudes of facts, that things were not what they were supposed to have been. Census reports are used to prove that the number of planters who owned a hundred slaves was small; that plantation houses were more often like factories than like Walter Scott's castles; that beautiful maidens were then not more numerous than they are now. Some historians are at pains to prove that the ancestors were not Virginia gentlemen and that the predecessors of the ancestors were not knights. Numerous investigators accuse the colonial Virginians of being ordinary persons. James Branch Cabell, with a vicious glee, befouls the nests of the forefathers by creating a repulsive age of chivalry.

Some Southern historians would change a belief which both friend and foe have taught us to think was the essence of the Old South. They tell us that the distinctions between aristocracy and humble folk were not so great as was once supposed; thereby would they take away from the aristocracy many of the distinctions of superior position. They tell us that the poor whites were not so numerous as was once supposed and that there was a substantial middle class which had no reason to feel inferior to the planter aristocracy. On the other hand, others, touched by twentieth-century concepts of human welfare, would let us know that the glory and glamor of the ante-bellum aristocracy was paid for by the humbling of the masses of both races.

A small shelf of books has been written by Southerners

proving that all Confederate soldiers were not brave and loyal Christian gentlemen; that in fact many of them were seditionists, draft dodgers, and deserters. To add to the disillusionment, Vann Woodward advances the belief that many of the brave and loyal veterans of the Confederate army did not possess common honesty. In page after page of interesting but disillusioning data, he parades paladins of the Confederacy from John B. Gordon to Basil Duke as a second generation of scalawags who robbed the land they professed to love.

This revision of Southern legends is based upon much research in manuscripts and other original documents. But the facts that can be unearthed by research in as complex a subject as human behavior are so infinite in extent that one set of data can refute another set. The masters of research, for example, have for a generation or two been digging up data to prove whether or not the gentry of Virginia are descended from King Charles's Cavaliers. The evidence is so varied, and the English and Southern methods of computing aristocratic descent so different, that the reader has not yet been able to draw conclusions.

Sometimes Southern historians forget that what is often important to Southerners is not what actually happened but what is believed to have happened. Southerners want their historians to do them concrete good by revealing or creating ancestors for them. An ironic fact about Southern historical writing is that the only practitioners of the craft able to make a living from their efforts are the genealogists. Their unique vice or virtue is that they are able to dig up useful ancestors where there may have been none before. Such discoveries give a person of declining fortunes a satisfaction not unlike the consolations of religion or philosophy. Such discoveries,

on the other hand, give persons of energy and ambition something with which to justify their assumptions of social and
civic worth.

Disillusioning researches in the records of the South's past
have not generally impressed the Southern people. This sort
of revelation must go unheeded if the South is to survive as a
cultural entity.

Donald Davidson says that the key to Southern literary
greatness is not the literature of protest but "the literature of
acceptance." Obedience to this standard, Mr. Davidson believes, is why the Southern imaginative literature of our times
is appreciated by the critics and the reading public. William
Faulkner, Eudora Welty, and Robert Penn Warren write in
the most modern manner; at times their stories are sordid.
They tell everything good and bad about the South. They
only reject what Davidson calls "the false knowledge" of
ignoring or deploring aspects of Southern life and character.
They are not, like so many of our historians, narrow demo-
crats and nationalists who measure the South's past by the
values of educated Americans of today.

The standards of accuracy demanded of the Southern historian are so exacting that he is often frightened out of writing a book because he must face the holy terror of having his
errors of fact exposed by well-intentioned reviewers. A strange
sense of reticence prevents him from telling a tale which
may be a revelation of the truth about the teller and his people. Think of the fate of one of our historians if he were to
join one of Faulkner's characters in asserting that our mulat-
toes were descendants of Yankee soldiers and carpetbaggers.
The Southern novelist is more concerned with the meaning
of events than with the technical accuracy of their recording.
He heeds the legends, the undying superstitions and prej-

udices of the people. His willingness and ability to use these in his tales is where his genius lies.

Southern historians often ignore the poor whites, rationalize them out of existence, or treat them as fit subjects for social-welfare programs. The novelists, on the other hand, portray them without apology or gratuitous sympathy and endow them with pride and humor. William Faulkner gives us a mob of country folk too chivalric to push aside a lady guard in order to lynch a Negro.

Religion as a constructive force in Southern life is generally unappreciated by our historians except for what it has done for education and social progress. Christian Fundamentalists are scolded for their capture of the Southern mind in the early nineteenth century and for their interference in science and politics in the twentieth century. The great Baptist church is tactfully ignored because, perhaps, it is an example of the union of Southern democracy with absolutism too indelicate and lusty for believers in Jeffersonian democracy. On the other hand, the novelists possess an affecting sympathy for the traditional religion. Ellen Glasgow in *Vein of Iron* and William Faulkner in *Light in August,* for example, demonstrate a tender understanding of Southern clergymen who were persecuted by their congregations.

Vann Woodward in *Origins of the New South* complains of the lack of understanding among Southern historians of the strain of violence which runs through Southern history. If measured at all by our historians, it is in terms of civics textbooks. Violence, on the other hand, is a dominant theme in Southern fiction. There murderous gentlemen and outlaws are presented with compassion and explained in terms of grand tragedy.

The historian of the South should join the social novelist

who accepts the values of the age and the section about which
he writes. He should learn to identify truth with legend and
with faith as competently as he has learned to identify truth
with facts. By mixing sympathy, understanding, and a bit of
kindness with his history, he might attract the people about
whom he writes to read his books. And this could be done
without sacrificing scholarly integrity.

Not all historians who rise above the level of scholarly com-
pilations are ashamed of the peculiar standards of their section. Some of them write "the literature of accommodation."
The Southern historian who has won the greatest applause
writes of the heroes of the Confederacy without arguing
whether or not they were quixotic. The best recognized historian of the Old South pictures plantation life without assuming that it was a grand mistake. Another historian ex-
amines the literature on the poor whites without moralizing
against them because they were not as thrifty as their social
betters. A recent historian of the New South joins William
Faulkner in exposing the true tragedy of the South: it was
not the defeat at Appomattox, but the truckling of both scala-
wag and Bourbon, both materialist and idealist, to alien
values.

⤲〜⤳

TWO

THE SOUTH'S DEMOCRATIC POSE

THE greatest mistake of a leader of the Old South was
Thomas R. Dew's choice of a European country in which
to be educated. The inaugurator of the Proslavery Argument,
who was president of William and Mary College, went to
Germany instead of to England. Had he gone to England he
would have been influenced by a society which proclaimed
the virtues of democracy and equality while it practiced social distinctions greater than elsewhere in Christendom. This
indulgence in what the French call "Anglo-Saxon hypocrisy"
paid off handsomely. The progressive world, kind enough to
accept a nation's evaluation of itself, believed the flattering
conceit that England was Europe's most democratic country,
that King and Lords were almost stage characters, not the top
of a social pyramid.

Had Dew been trained in England, he could have returned
home talking of freedom and democracy while covertly ac-
cepting the inherited realities of slavery and agrarian aristocracy. Such a shrewd unwillingness to reconcile theory with

reality would have led disagreeable Europeans to cry, "pur-
poseful absentmindedness"; but there is reason to believe that
the forces of democracy and liberalism, in their greed for
conquest, might not have regarded the Old South as an
enemy. The outside world might have been credulous enough
to accept the region of slavery according to its profession of
democratic sweetness and evolutionary light. The world's
evaluation of Thomas Jefferson and Abraham Lincoln proves
that this was possible.

Jefferson represented himself as the champion of simplicity, equality, and modesty. So successful was this pose that
he is accepted as a guide by all advocates of democracy from
Wall Street bankers to communists; he is one of the few
Americans who cannot be criticized successfully. Yet he was
not too simple to live in a Roman mansion instead of in a log
cabin and to drink madeira wine instead of hard cider. He
was not too freedom- and equality-loving to profit by the
labor of slaves. He was not too modest to rationalize God
into an image strikingly resembling Mr. Jefferson himself.

Abraham Lincoln, because of his black beard and white
face, looked like St. John the Baptist; in proclaiming "charity
to all men," he talked like an humble servant of mankind. At
this evaluation he is universally accepted. Yet he was un-
charitable enough to wish the Negroes to banish themselves
from the land as a condition of their freedom, and was determined to accomplish the great act of national unification
over the bodies of thousands.

Dew went to Germany where he learned from Aristotle-
inspired professors that all men are not equal and that slavery
is as natural as freedom. On coming home he coupled this
information with the Bible to justify the keeping of the black
man in bondage. Negro slavery, this Southerner asserted, was

a necessity of social decency in a community where black men were numerous. There was no hiding of practices and intentions. As applied to the Negro the Jeffersonian doctrine of freedom and equality was denied. Dew and his proslavery successors conjured up one hundred arguments to answer the ninety-nine arguments the pundits of democracy were able to collect.

The defenders of the peculiar ways of the Old South were mistaken in believing that they could win the argument through the mere weight of superior logic. The advocates of democracy could use force as readily as reason. They shot down all the targets their proslavery antagonists put before them. The South was subjected to the bloodiest assault in modern history before 1914. The region below the Potomac went down in tragic defeat. It paid the penalty of foolishly assuming that revolutionists prating Jefferson believed that truth expressed in words was the most effective weapon against error. Slave-whippers should have known that liberals also can be violent.

The South learned its lesson in 1865. It relegated Dew and his group to the limbo of history and rejoined other Americans in proclaiming the Jeffersonian doctrines which it had professed in the early years of the Republic. This was not enough. To these inherited verities, Southern leaders of the postwar generation added democratic doctrines suited to the new day. They created the myth of the New South by championing universal education and the introduction of Northern industry and Northern ideals of a business civilization. They asserted that the South, in harmony with the benign optimism of Herbert Spencer, would, if given time, shelve its sectionalism and evolve into a happy segment of the great republic in which plutocracy and democracy stood united.

Booker T. Washington, the most eminent Southerner of his day, was applauded. He possessed a plan, devious but thoroughly American and materialistic, which promised to raise his race out of the slough of caste into the equality which the Reconstruction experiment had failed to achieve. A Southern congressman was willing to eulogize Charles Sumner. Ex-rebel generals in 1898 were willing to put on the blue uniform and march under the flag they had fought against three decades before. Give the South a bit of the immense time the Victorians allotted to the evolutionary process and it would give up its dark and lackadaisical ways, with only a few magnolias and colonnaded porches left as relics of a benighted past.

Such professions, however, did not square with practice. The statesman who eulogized Sumner had already broken the jaw of a carpetbagger in the Mississippi county whose dark ways William Faulkner was destined to expose. The South was learning to supplement a revived American patriotism with a fervent reassertion of regional consciousness. It sublimated Jefferson into the aristocrat he truly was. It resented the aspersion that the wife of Andrew Jackson, its most democratic leader, smoked a pipe. It countered Booker T. Washington's optimism by indulging in lynching, job-expulsions, jim-crowing, and disfranchising. It negated the democratic nationalism of the schools by home influences with a Southern bias. It filled the new factory towns with persons as rural in their thinking as those left on the farms. And when, through force bills, office-giving, and civil rights programs, Northern leaders threatened reenactment of the Reconstruction experiment, the South was bitter.

Perhaps the propagandists of post-bellum democracy knew that their words did not reflect the Southern reality. But if they dissimulated, they were lying like the diplomats and gentlemen they were. And they knew that the North was sharing their guilt, even indulging in democratic hypocrisy. They observed that the District of Columbia preferred to lose the sacred privileges of self-government and legislative representation rather than have Negroes participate in the process. They knew that proclamations by New York City and Chicago in favor of race equality were accompanied by the relegation of Negroes to ghettos. They knew that carpet-baggers had not married Negroes and that Yankee school-ma'ams at Berea College, in Kentucky, chaperoned so effectively their only successful Southern experiment in interracial education that there were no chances for much interracial familiarities. They knew that the twentieth-century Presidents of the United States as late as 1960 did not practice their preachments against race discriminations. They noted that these high officials did not fraternize with Negroes while in the South; that they failed to appoint Negroes to public office in the South; that they did not invoke the Fourteenth Amendment's provisions allowing the reduction of representation in Congress as the most effective method of frustrating the South's habit of reducing Negro participation in politics to a minimum. Southerners got sardonic delight over the curbs imposed upon a President's wife who awkwardly believed that the discriminations Americans imposed upon thirteen million Negroes should be compared with the discriminations the Germans imposed upon eight hundred thousand Jews.

Oswald Spengler explains the marvelous internal order of the United States in terms of the harmony which exists between plutocracy and democracy. The poor, for reasons that are obvious, admire the rich more than the rich admire them-

selves. In the South this principle is modified by the sub-
stitution of the aristocratic for the money concept.

Historians are disappointed when they look in the Old
South for evidences of the Marxian stereotype of the class
struggle. They find instead a close conformity by all classes
to the concept of broad acres, many slaves, and the colonnaded mansion. The common white man resented Hinton
R. Helper's assertion in his *Impending Crisis of the South*
(1857) that all the people were handicapped economically
and socially by the planters and the slaves. So odd do Helper's
views appear in the environment of the Old South that one
historian declared that he was under German influence. The
aristocratic consciousness of the white masses of this civilization found unhappy expression in laws of growing rigidity
for the control of the slaves and in a dangerous greed for the
possession of lands on which they might fulfill their desire to
be slaveholders. It found pleasing expression in the sense of
mannerliness which pervaded all classes of Southern society.

The aristocratic concept has been so compelling a factor
in the development of the New South that it is difficult to discover institutions of wide popular approval of lower-class
origin. The most striking exception to this rule is jazz music,
an activity which started in the Negro quarter of New Orleans and ultimately entered the ball rooms of the rich and
the wellborn. Another exception is the leftovers from hog
killings such as spareribs and pig's feet which have been
metamorphosed by colored cooks into delicacies for the lady's
table. A third exception is the mellowing of the corn whisky
of the backwoodsman into the bourbon whisky of the gentleman.

The social history of the South is largely the story of the
masses imitating their social betters. The aristocratic ideal

stands, as Wilbur J. Cash says in *The Mind of the South,* "perpetually suspended in the great haze of memory, . . . poised somewhere between earth and sky, colossal, shining, and incomparably lovely." It expresses itself in the interests of the thousands of ladies who between the Potomac and the Rio Grande endlessly contemplate their forebears; in the linking of many persons of any degree of sophistication with slave barons; in the penchant in the newer suburbs for domestic architecture which extends beyond colonial Virginia into Tudor England; and in the attraction of hundreds of thousands to Colonial Williamsburg and to Natchez. A primary reason for the failure of the second Ku Klux Klan is that the upper classes divested the order of its knightly pretensions and exposed it as a clique of barbers, small farmers, and mechanics. An important reason why labor unions have made less progress in the South than elsewhere is that they have never been associated with the upper classes. Pride in social distinctions made the South reluctant to accept woman suffrage. This also has much to do with the fact that the success of the Dixie demagogues was seldom lasting. The South is normally satisfied with political leaders who are gentlemen or at least have gentlemanly aspirations.

The region between the Potomac and the Rio Grande has a larger proportion of its population in church than any other section of the United States. But about its religious bodies are class distinctions which alarm believers in the brotherhood of man. There is one church for the whites and another for the blacks; one for a certain class who are Episcopalians; one for another class who are Baptists; one for a third class who are Holy Rollers. The Catholic minority is sometimes despised because it is of Irish or other non-Anglo-Saxon origin. The Baptists are often disparaged by the socially secure and the socially ambitious because this popular church is less selective than the Episcopalians and the Presbyterians. Among the Baptists themselves congregations are organized along social lines. There is a Baptist church for Mill Town; a second for business and professional people; and a third for Nigger Town.

The loose assertion of historians that the Baptist church is of lower class origin is not sustained by the evidence. In Virginia and North Carolina, where this denomination was first introduced around 1760, it won at first only a small minority; they were persons who were not, as were the Episcopalians and Presbyterians, aristocrats; but they were not of the lower classes. Unlike the Anabaptists of Germany, the Southern Baptists accepted the leadership of educated New Englanders and of aristocrats like Madison and Jefferson. Although accused by those who did not understand them of revolutionary ambitions, they accepted the inherited standards of Virginia in social and economic matters.

Public education is the most widely accorded social privilege of the states of the New South. By 1950 its benefits were extended to all children of both races. Yet it was not the common people who inaugurated this system. It was the dispensation of upper-class agitators and state bureaucrats upon the local communities. Its objective has been the elevation of the common people to aristocratic levels. It imposes cultural standards superior to those of the ancestors.

The Negro, whom Gunnar Myrdal calls an exaggerated American, is the perfect Southerner. He imitates his social superiors among the Southern whites. On winning his liberty, he did not revert to forms of barbarism either American or African. Instead he took the white man's name, his religion, and his social customs. His women developed a passion for finery. He went to schools where his mentors expected him to recover industrial skills in keeping with his humble opportunities; instead he devoted himself to the arts esteemed by the white upper classes.

In the aristocratic aspirations of Southerners are elements of snobbery. In Northern Virginia hunting is practiced in the English style rather than in the style natural to America. Despite broad professions of democracy, Texans are not too humble to imitate the English and Virginians in this respect. The advance of the automobile as the most convenient method of conveyance has not prevented the expansion of horsemanship among the socially ambitious. The growth of the Episcopalian and Presbyterian churches in recent years was caused in part by social advantages accruing to their members. Vast expenditures of the Southern states for education in the humbler trades and professions have not led the carpenter's son to return to the work bench or the farmer's son to return to the plow. Education, if not the means of learning how to get more by doing less, is a means of aspiring after the elevating occupations. The stenographer has learned to dress like the society girl. Golf, once the diversion of the banker, has been taken up by the bank clerk. Football, once only interesting to the college student, is now a main interest of the city workingman.

The Southerner in his actual living accepts the assertion that there "are all sorts and conditions of men." He could, if he would, justify this attitude by appeals to seers less ancient than Aristotle and the Elizabethans. From modern psychology he could learn that individual differences rather than equality is the rule of nature. From Theodore Dreiser's *An American Tragedy,* as explained by English reviewers, he could learn that something is fundamentally wrong with a society which allows a youth to aspire after a position beyond his training and intelligence. The reason he hates Soviet Russia is that he sees disadvantages in the extension of social equality into unaccustomed fields: wealth, dress, and occupations. He could learn that the shortcoming of his expensive school system can be explained partly in terms of applying the same training to all children regardless of actual distinction in talents and backgrounds. He could contemplate the fact that the esthetic barrenness of his section can be explained by the democratic monotony made possible by modern technology and education.

The Southerner could read in both American and European sources the lesson that the key to progress is the existence of an elite. Thomas Carlyle taught it again and again. The Southerner could learn that Europe's great cultural advances from the Renaissance to the present were upper class impositions. Would there, for example, have been an English literature had there been no English aristocracy? He might realize that one of the causes of American progress is the existence of a social ladder which the ambitious person wishes to climb rather than tear down.

The Southerner, whatever he may say in his formal moments, does not wish the type of democracy envisaged by the Declaration of Independence and expressed in the Fourteenth and Fifteenth Amendments. Actually he wishes to maintain a caste system more rigid than any which has ever existed in Europe. Why? Because he believes this caste system has been the means of conserving the purity of the white race during the 344 years in which this race has been in contact with the African race. He knows that other white Americans, whatever arguments to the contrary they may gather from anthropology, accept the same view, although he may grant that the anthropologists are correct in asserting the innate mental equality of all races.

To the South Robert E. Lee is a more precious symbol than Thomas Jefferson. It is the difference between the defeated gentleman in immaculate uniform and jeweled sword and the triumphant democrat who looked like "a tall, large rawboned farmer" and demonstrated his simplicity by wearing ill-fitting, much worn clothes. This preference makes possible the existence among Southerners of their single unique virtue. It is a certain courtliness of manner which makes all men in a sense into gentlemen. In this attitude is a certain amount of romantic ineffectiveness; but in it is room for an ideal of precious worth for a world tending to be dominated by the communist materialism of Russia and the capitalist materialism of the United States.

Why does the South not divest itself of its democratic pretenses about race and class in order to justify its real passion for social distinctions? Thereby it might be at ease with the compelling forces of its ancient heritage. Thereby it might repel the accusation of hypocritical pose and enjoy the comfort of preaching what it intends to do. But the region below the Potomac is not likely to change its evasive habits. It remembers the price of its frankness in 1861. It knows that the meddlesome Yankee is using a confession of sins against Jefferson as a pretext for starting a second Reconstruction. Recent Federal court decisions and Federal legislative proposals give substance to this threat.

These fears should not be so great. Changes which the armies of Grant and Sherman were not able to effect can scarcely be brought about by judicial or legislative ukase. The United States is a federal republic with ingrained sentiments in favor of local determination in matters of intimate concern. Revolutionary changes in the Southern social structure are implied by the plans for Fair Labor Practice and for the abolition of biracial schools; they could be made effective only by the change of the United States into a police state. Such absolutism, even to promote the Jeffersonian dream, is not part of the liberal tradition of America.

THREE

THE SOUTH AS A REGION

Europe influence is the principal factor in American greatness—a greatness which could not have been realized without modifying this influence to meet the hardships and opportunities of a new land. Settlers in the North partly solved this problem by establishing themselves in American climates like those from which they came. Settlers in the South, on the other hand, were forced to face the problems of the semitropics. Because of this, the sufferings of the early Southerners were great. "The low and marshy ground, the hot sun, the unwholesome drinking water," says Virginian Thomas Wertenbaker, "combined to produce an unending epidemic of dysentery and malaria."

Adjustments to the climate of the South have enabled immigrants from North Europe to live and multiply there for 356 years. E. N. Vallandigham, a geographer, writes, "Not elsewhere the world over have Englishmen dwelt continuously in large numbers under semi-tropical conditions for so much as three generations." Southerners did this, maintaining the English way of life to as great a degree as any group of Americans.

The Southerner's problem of modifying European habits to fit the New World was followed by a similar problem: adopting benefits derived from the booming civilization of the northern half of the United States without abandoning progress in making adjustments to the Southern environment. While winning its cultural and social independence from England, the region below the Potomac had to struggle against the tendency to become a colonial dependency of the North. Northern customs were in many respects more alluring than those of the mother country. England represented past glories; the region above the Potomac represented progress—a level of material wealth and democratic idealism greater than anywhere in Europe. The South achieved much progress through imitating the North. It learned to use Northern machines, Northern literature, art, and education, and Northern political reforms. But the pull forward of the Yankee spirit was no more successful in destroying the Southern qualities than the pull backward of the mother country in preventing Southern qualities from developing. There is, said Donald Davidson in 1938, the reality of regionalism acknowledged in the vocabulary of the people if not in the solemn documentations of statesmen.

The American devotion to centralization has not, Davidson adds, "stirred the Rockies from their base, or unchannelled the Mississippi, or removed the plains, the lakes, the climate itself." The geographical diversity which these factors create divides America into a variety of sections, of which the South is the most distinct. There the winter is neither very long nor very cold; in summer for fifty afternoons the temperature climbs to ninety degrees in the shade; throughout the year there is greater humidity, more sunshine, and less wind than elsewhere in the United States. At certain seasons there are torrential rains, and along the Gulf of Mexico the growing season lasts nine months.

These marks of sun, rain and wind exert gross as well as subtle influences. Long, hot seasons favored the creation of the kingdoms of tobacco, rice, sugar, and cotton; slowed down the tempo of living and of speech; promoted outdoor life; modified architecture to make indoor living cooler; and encouraged the employment of Negroes on the land. The poorer soils, eroded and leached by heavy rains, gave white and black alike excuse for poverty and leisure.

Geography, coupled with the complications of social development, makes possible the recognition of distinctive features in Southern civilization. The doctrine of white supremacy, asserts the historian Ulrich B. Phillips, is "the central theme" of Southern history. In the presence of large masses of blacks, the white people developed a superior and unique attitude toward the other race. This attitude, according to Phillips, is the essence of Southernism. To white supremacy, Avery O. Craven adds another explanation—the prevalence of the country-gentleman ideal, a pattern of society borrowed from the English, justified by the physiocratic philosophy of the French, and taking root naturally in the agricultural South. The poet John Crowe Ransom regards Southernism as the creation, by the men of the Old South, of the ideal of a conservative civilization which "put the surplus energy in the free life of the mind" and which gave scope to the refinements of settled life in rural comfort. By others, Southernism has been variously attributed to the fundamental piety of the people, their emphasis on home life, the peculiarities of their food, the survival of their rural ways even in growing cities, a powerful nativism largely untouched within the past 187 years by immigration, and the survival of the Southern type of lady and gentleman, who Count Hermann Keyserling declared to be "the only types of 'complete souls' that the United States has yet produced."

Many observers admit that Southernism is a reality too elusive to be explained in objective terms. It is something like a song or an emotion, more easily felt than recorded. "Poets have done better in expressing the oneness of the South," remarks James G. Randall, "than historians in explaining it." One of the characters in George W. Cable's *John March, Southerner* speaks of "a certain ungeographical South-within-the-South—as portable and intangible as the souls in our bodies." In exile in the iron cold of New England, Quinton Compson is asked, "Why do you hate the South?" "I don't hate it," William Faulkner has him say in *Absalom, Absalom!* "I don't hate it," he repeats. *"I don't hate it,* he thinks; *I don't! I don't hate it! I don't hate it!"*

A wealth of imaginative literature and factual scholarship have described the Old South as contrasted with the Old North. There is the difference between the land of the Cavalier and of the Puritan, of slavery and of freedom, of agriculture and of industry, of planter and of small farmer, of static contentment and of progressive aspiration. Contemporaries were so aware of the sectional differences that they spoke of two nations as distinct as France and England, with a congress at Washington, not to discuss common interests, but to proclaim mutual grievances.

Beginning in the 1820's, Southerners recognized the realities of sectional divergences by developing a social and political philosophy. Slavery, the region's most distinctive institution, once regarded as an embarrassing necessity, was interpreted as conferring positive benefits on all elements of Southern society. It was justified by arguments drawn from the Bible, from Aristotle, and from what was accepted as science. The relation between master and servant was explained as a bond made in heaven along with the bond of the human family. The proslavery argument was so cunningly combined with American ideals that servitude appeared the very condition of democracy. Since the Negro was made for manual labor, white skin protected the individual who was not a slave against social degradation. The ideal state was that of the slave master and his lady, who found a mirror of their lives in the chivalric society of the Middle Ages.

The North was adjudged guilty of attempting, through the tyranny of the majority, to impose unbearable hardships upon the minority section. These hardships were protective tariffs, building means of transportation at Federal expense, adopting commercial strategies through which Southern wealth went into Northern pockets, weakening slavery through harboring fugitives, keeping slaves out of Western territories, and agitating for the ultimate abolition of slavery. To protect themselves against these acts of aggression, the Southerners evolved the doctrine of States' Rights. This took at first the form of threatened or actual nullification by the states of acts of the Federal government, and the suggestion of a system of concurrent majorities through which the weaker section might veto the acts of the stronger. When these devices failed, Southerners asserted the right to withdraw from the Federal Union.

The distinctiveness of the Old South is perhaps best illustrated by its religion. Historic Protestantism was reduced to the consistencies of the Southern environment without sacrificing inherent fundamentals. Religious revivals lifted the

common people out of frontier indifference to religion. The
discipline of church schools held Southerners of both races in
the Christian communions. The Southern mind, which at the
beginning of the nineteenth century had been under the influence of liberal deists, was captured for the orthodoxies by
an aggressive group of revivalists. Both church- and state-
controlled colleges were dedicated to the "old-time religion."
These changes prepared the way for the complete reconciliation between slavery and the Southern churches, for breaking
ties with the antislavery churches of the North, and for use
among the Negroes of the bondage of the soul as a means of
making more secure the bondage of the body. On Biblical
grounds, the Ethiopian was declared to be the descendant of
Ham, fated to be the hewer of wood and the drawer of water.
He solaced himself with the development of sacred songs
proclaiming the joys of heaven as compensation for the tribu-
lations of slavery.

Historians, in their efforts to explain the coming of the
Civil War, emphasize the differences between the Old South
and the Old North. They forget that conflicts can be as easily
explained in terms of similarities as well as differences. Perhaps the American Civil War was another example of Greek
meeting Greek, of Anglo-Saxon quarreling with Anglo-
Saxon with the same ideals and ambitions. The fight began in
Kansas, where two groups of Americans used the controversy
over slavery as an excuse for struggle to possess the land. Both
sides, with Anglo-Saxon shrewdness, whipped out Bibles and
guns to justify their desires.

The society of the Old South, like that of the Old North,
was given to expansion both horizontally and perpendic-
ularly. Horizontal expansion for the Southerner meant fre-
quent migration westward; even the slave was not a peasant

tied to the soil. Perpendicular expansion meant that humble men could rise to the top. It was possible, says historian of the Old South, Charles Sydnor, for men to mount "from log cabin to plantation mansion on a stairway of cotton bales, accumulating slaves as they climbed." This process was easy because of an expanding society and because of the relative absence of class lines. The dominance of all white men over the Negro created a sense of brotherhood not unlike the Greek concept of democracy. Universal white manhood suffrage was established in all Southern states. In the persons of John Randolph, William L. Yancey, and Albert G. Brown, the Dixie demagogue was almost as important as he was destined to be in the days of Ben Tillman and Theodore G. Bilbo. Education for all white children was progressively applied; to the Prussian purpose of using the school to promote skills and discipline, was added, without reluctance, the American notion of the school as an instrument for ironing out social distinctions.

Abraham Lincoln was correct in assuming that no impassable barrier could be erected between the sections. The Old South did not have the will or the resources for national self-expression. It had no political, economic, or cultural capital. It was dependent upon the North for manufactured articles, cloth made from its cotton, styles for women's clothes, the books and the magazines it read, and the textbooks and many of the teachers of its schools. Bitterly did Southern writers like James D. B. De Bow complain of the high prices the North was able to charge for its goods; but the commercial and cultural conventions of the 1850's for the purpose of creating regional autonomy had scant success. The fact that a national soul did not survive the defeat of 1865 makes one wonder if such a soul ever existed.

The Old South of these enumerated differences and contrasts was defeated at Appomattox. In its place was created a New South, in which slavery was abolished and in which industrialization and sectional reconciliation became aspirations. The South's central problem was to adjust its standards to those of the victorious North. As the result of war and Reconstruction, it recognized the supremacy of the Union, free Negro labor, and the equality of all men before the law. Later the national ideals of business success and industrial advance won victories over the agrarian tradition; and the New South demonstrated in practice the New England concept of universal education. Imported views on religion and science were accepted by college-bred leaders; imported class alignments and recreations altered social life. In deference to the critical standards of metropolitan areas, the South created a literature that affronted its romantic pride. Despite a painful sensitivity, it allowed the Negro to progress along lines consistent with Northern concepts of uplift. And with unrestrained patriotism, Southerners participated in the battles of three national wars and in the councils of four national administrations. Because of these concessions to Northern standards, there was basis for the conclusion that by 1930 the states of the former Confederacy had so far receded from the sectionalism of 1861 that they were about to become a mere segment of a unified republic.

To justify this progression out of an unhappy past, there arose a group of publicists known as the Southern Liberals. In the name of a liberal tradition said to be as inherently Southern as Thomas Jefferson, the Southern Liberals assaulted religious orthodoxy, puritanism, demagoguery, rural conservatism, and other aspects of the Southern scene. They were modern enough to advocate state action in social and economic fields quite beyond the Jeffersonian concept of an agrarian society. They advocated libraries, good roads, hospitals, school expansion, and other such material comforts as the common people in all progressive societies demand of their rulers.

The capital blunder of the leaders of the Old South was their emphasis upon slavery as an explanation of the sectional variations. This accent upon a despised institution brought upon the region the charge of bloodguilt and led its enemies to compel the tragic exorcism of 1865. The leaders of the New South, once the conquerors had relented enough to allow the restoration of white supremacy, did not pursue a policy which brought upon them a second civil war. They did not try to restore the old order. Under their direction the truly forgotten men of Southern history became Thomas R. Dew and the other writers who proclaimed the inequality of man as the prime justification of slavery. The Jeffersonian dream of the equality of all men became a Southern axiom. About this declaration was much unreality. Leaders of the New South such as Henry W. Grady and Charles B. Aycock pressed for the disfranchisement of the blacks and at the same time preached "glittering generalities" about progress and democracy. Nevertheless, they were not sweepingly reactionary toward the Negro. They allowed him schools, religious freedom, and the right to own property and to move away. This was because, as Gunnar Myrdal sapiently observes, the Southern white man had learned to adhere so deeply to the American creed of democracy that his conscience did not permit extreme actions against the Negro or the denial to him of hope of more equalities in the future.

So much emphasis has been placed on the willingness of the South to move out of its past that a legend of greatest practical importance has been created. It is believed that the region is in a constant state of change which will ultimately result in the annihilation of the sectional differences in order that it may embrace all the benefits of the national life. "Everywhere," said Louis M. Hacker and Benjamin B. Kendrick, two competent chroniclers of the national annals in 1932, "the South gave way before the onrush of the North. . . . It would not be stretching too much to say that before the nineteenth century closed the South had become a mere appendage of New York or the Ohio Valley." This great change has been implemented by the bulldozing of much of the Southern landscape out of its original shape to make clearings for Northern-owned industries. Its reality has been accepted so thoroughly by the spokesmen of the South that Harvard scholar Paul H. Buck, was able to use their words as the basis of a book detailing the growth of sectional amity.

The legend of the changing South has been, from time to time, the basis for optimistic thinkers to assume the actual or imminent solution of the problems which make the section different. It was possible for Frederick Douglass to assume as early as 1879 that conditions in the Southern States were so steadily improving "that the colored man will ultimately realize the fullest measure of liberty and equality accorded and secured in any section of our common country." James W. Garner asserted in 1914 that the time had come for the section "to emancipate herself from the deadly one-party system" because the question of Negro suffrage for the indefinite future had been settled by disfranchising amendments to state constitutions. The legend reached its ultimate extreme in a book written by Edwin Mims in 1926 entitled *The Advancing South* and containing a chapter called "The Ebbing

Tide of Color." It survives today in the assertion of an Arkansas editor, Harry S. Ashmore, that the increased voting of Negroes in the Democratic primaries makes the race "a potent, positive factor in the region" and makes "the passing of the one-party system inevitable."

These sanguine hopes have not been fulfilled. The South has not given the Negro the liberty and equality accorded him elsewhere; the Negro question and the one-party system except in national elections have not been eliminated from politics; the color line has not broken down except in reluctant obedience to decrees of the Federal courts. Southern culture, as Donald Davidson said in 1938, "has an enormous vitality, even in those attitudes which sociologists call survivals: its ways of humor, its 'stubborn bantering threats to outsiders,' and various 'defense mechanisms.'" Numerous cultural factors, together with "a certain revivification of sectional antagonisms," declared the South's leading sociologist in 1936, Howard W. Odum, have "contributed to an apparent solidifying of the regional culture." These "sectional antagonisms" continued as late as 1963 to have a solidifying influence. There have been changes, but as Stark Young wisely observed in 1930, the changing South is still the South.

It is well to warn against the optimistic pronouncements of Southern progressives. Frequently they are rare specimens protected by aristocratic family connections or by the isolation of academic or editorial sanctums from the mass sentiments around them. Gunnar Myrdal scornfully noted in 1943 that the Southern liberal was afraid of "the deadly blow of being called a 'nigger lover'" and therefore liked to keep the Negro out of sight in agitations designed for the benefit of the race. Liberal pronouncements on a national or sectional level of group organizations are not likely to be implemented on local levels. Myrdal contrasted the bold words and actions of the central office of the National Association for the Advancement of Colored People with the timidity of this association's chapters in Southern towns. He also noted that white ministers are not likely to burden their congregations with the liberal exhortations on the race question which they are supposed to bring back from the general assemblies of their churches. When such exhortations are brought home, they are likely to lead to the expulsion of the minister. Observant persons realize the indifference of the thousands who each Sunday attend the Bible classes of the South to the liberal and even radical study materials which national church organizations put into their hands. "In the sphere of religion," Richard M. Weaver observes, "the Southerner has always been hostile to the spirit of inquiry. He felt that religion which is intellectual is not religion."

The facts do not justify the claim that the history of North-South relations since 1865 has been a record of steady decline in the intersectional asperities. An examination of the evidence reveals a series of ups and downs in an everlasting battle between the forces for sectional reconciliation and those for sectional estrangement.

The let-us-have-peace sentiments at Appomattox were followed by the hates of Reconstruction. Indeed, the bitterness created by the attempt to give Negroes some share of the American dream of equality was more lasting than that created by the antecedent bloodshed. The good will created by the surrender of the North in 1877 on the Reconstruction issue was matched by the ill will created by the Lodge Force Bill of 1890 and by the disfranchising amendments to the Southern state constitutions. The intersectional and interracial friendship created by Booker T. Washington was dimmed by the affronts of Theodore Roosevelt and the muck-rakers to the Southern standards of caste.

The sense of national pride engendered in Southern hearts by the election of Woodrow Wilson and the victories of World War I was followed by an attack on the South which Donald Davidson characterized as "more abusive and unrelenting than anything the Southern States have experienced since the last Federal soldier was withdrawn from their soil." There were Ku-Klux exposures, ridicule of Southern political and religious attitudes, and uncovering of alleged abuses of justice. The good will engendered between Franklin D. Roosevelt and the South was followed by legislation which affronted the traditions of the region. The willingness of the South to bear its share of the armed crusade to impose American ideals of equality upon Japan and Germany was followed by the demand that the South apply this ideal to the Negro. There was created an atmosphere of suspicion and alarm over Northern intentions. This alarm after 1954 was accentuated by decisions of the United States Supreme Court and by acts of the Eisenhower and Kennedy administrations.

In 1930 a group of twelve writers known as the Southern Agrarians supplemented a justification of the right of the South to maintain its historic identity with the belief that the South they esteemed was nearer the reality than the progressive South praised by the Liberals. The twelve understood that national standardization had not annihilated the fundamental differences of their section.

Even though the modern Southerner joins the Westerner and Northerner in adopting a common type of automobile, house, and clothes, he has not necessarily surrendered his distinctions of thought and emotions. Reading the same book and attending the same school do not necessarily eliminate

provincial thinking. The conversion of many educated Southerners to the logic of liberalism does not imply a willingness
to put aside inherited habits and to live according to the new
logic. Few of the many who talk against race prejudice are
willing to suffer the penalties of violating customary racial
barriers; few who believe that the cause of liberalism can be
promoted by having two political parties are willing to incur
the displeasure of their conservative neighbors by voting for
a political party in state and local affairs other than the Democratic.

Examination of many of the phases of the institutional life
of the New South reveals a constantly recurring condition:
despite the changes which the catastrophe of 1865 made inevitable, the distinctive culture of the section was never destroyed. In politics, to cite the most obvious example, the
South responded to the suggestion that the Negro be given
the equalities mentioned in the Declaration of Independence
by reducing the race to political impotence. The opening,
since 1937, of the Democratic primaries to the Negroes by the
Federal courts effected a change more technical than actual.
While there was a considerable increase in colored voters, the
new voters generally won the privilege of ratifying procedures
already determined by white majorities. An unchanging caste
system except in rare cases prevented the Negro from becoming a candidate for office or from effecting policies contrary
to the will of the whites. The sum total of his political gains
to date in the region below the Potomac are favors from
municipal authorities, one seat in the Georgia senate, and an
occasional member on a city council or a state board of education.

A lasting break in the political unity of the white race is
the fond hope of the friends of Negro uplift. Thereby would

it be possible for the minority race to hold the balance of power between white factions. Such a break has not come. It was threatened in 1928, when five states of the so-called Solid South voted against the Democratic candidate for President. When in the election of 1932 the name of the objectionable candidate was removed from the ballot, the Southern states voted unanimously for Democratic candidates and repudiated the leaders of the 1928 bolt. Again in 1948 was there a threat to political unity when the Southern people disapproved the desire of the Democratic presidential candidate to extend certain civil rights to Negroes. The people left to the leaders of the state machines the determination of the method to meet this emergency. In the majority of Southern states these leaders decreed that Southern interests could better be served by supporting the nominee of the traditional party; the voters fell in line. In four states the machine leaders felt that local interests could better be served by supporting an independent candidate; the voters fell in line. In subsequent Presidential elections Southern states in limited numbers voted Republican but continued to vote Democratic on state and local issues. Thus in no Southern state was white solidarity sufficiently broken to make the Negro vote of first importance.

Although concessions were made to the liberal spirit in regard to the Negro, the South remained adamant in the matter of greatest importance. The bonds of caste, by which the Negro was kept subordinate and underprivileged, were weakened in few respects. In the middle of the twentieth century it was still possible for the demagogue to win office by campaigning against Negro rights; for whites to take jobs away from blacks when members of the superior caste desired them; for business opportunities and employment in the newer industries to be white monopolies; and for Negroes for all practical purposes to be excluded from the professions of politics, law, and engineering. The average white still has three tones in his voice: a normal tone for whites; a "mammy voice" for Negroes with whom he is familiar; and a haughty tone for strange Negroes. The achievement of the blacks in the mixing of the races in schools and in agencies of public transportation was brought about by detested Federal courts and other agents of benevolent Northerners, only to a limited degree, through the efforts of the Negroes themselves. The major equality which the blacks won for themselves is the right to migrate North, to move from job to job, from country to town. Negro students, protected by the isolation of college communities from white control, have through "sit-down" strikes won for themselves the right to sit at lunch counters in a number of Southern cities.

Since the Civil War, there has been a steady decline in what the ante-bellum traveler Frederick Law Olmsted called "the close cohabitation and association of black and white." Immediately after the war the two races separated in churches, and for the cultural give and take of the plantation was substituted a dual school system which sealed off the children of one race from the other. Gradually it became impossible for a white person to teach in a Negro school without losing caste. When the courts forced the attendence of Negroes in white schools, no genuine interracial fraternity developed. No longer did the two races have what William Faulkner calls "the same parties: the identical music from identical instruments, crude fiddles and guitars, now in the big house with candles and silk dresses and champagne, now in the dirt-floored cabins with smoking pine knots and calico and water sweetened with molasses." The whites have been able to implement a growing aversion to intimate contact with the blacks through the use of labor-saving devices and through the spread of progressive notions concerning the dignity of labor. Despite Supreme Court decisions, immutable social custom makes for increased residential segregation, especially in the newer sections of the cities. In two of the newer cities of Virginia, Virginia Beach and Colonial Heights, there are no Negro residents. In many places the blacks live so far away from white settlements that the whites find it impractical to hire them as servants. In fewer numbers are blacks sitting in the balconies of white theaters or patronizing white physicians and dentists. It is now almost possible for a middle-class person to live many years in a Southern city without contact with blacks.

One of the most persistent beliefs about the South is that the Negro is in a constant state of revolt against the social pattern of the section. Despite a vast literature to the contrary, the facts of history refute this assumption. As a slave the black man never attempted general insurrection and did not run away often. "The slaves," says a historian of the Confederacy, Robert Cotterill, "supported the war unanimously (albeit somewhat involuntarily)." It is now proved that outside compulsions rather than inner ambitions prompted the political insubordinations of Reconstruction. Their artificial character is proved by the fact that they were not accompanied by much social insubordinations and by the fact that they disappeared as soon as the outside compulsions were removed. Indicative of the willingness of the rank and file of the blacks to accept the status quo are the words of a conservative demagogue who knew the Negro well. If the election of the governor of South Carolina were left "entirely to the Negro vote," declared Cole L. Blease in 1913, "I would receive without trouble 75 to 90 per cent." In communities in Virginia, North Carolina, and

Tennessee where the blacks have made wide use of the suffrage, there have been social and economic gains for the race
but no effective assault on white supremacy. This fact is one
of the main arguments advanced by Southern Liberals in
favor of giving the blacks the suffrage. Of late, the prospective
Negro voters have abandoned the comparatively independent
Republican party in order to join a party dominated by their
white neighbors. They vote, not for the Henry Wallaces and
others who practice race equality, but for those who at best
render only lip service to this principle.

That the Negroes are not in revolt against the white pattern
of civilization is illustrated by their conduct in a field of action
in which they possess almost perfect freedom: religion. They
voluntarily imitate the whites in this. They join the whites in
maintaining the orthodoxies and in creating a black counterpart to almost every one of the white denominations. If the
masses of the whites are Baptists, so are the masses of the
blacks; if the upper-class whites are Episcopalians or Presbyterians, so are the upper-class blacks. If the Catholics, Uni-
tarians, and Congregationalists make little headway among
the whites, the same is true among the blacks. If skepticism
and atheism make little appeal to Southern whites, the same is
true of the Southern blacks. Among them there is no relapse
into paganism, either African or of other types. The Black
Muslim movement of recent years has made little headway in
the South outside the columns of newspapers. The lessons
taught from the Bible by the slave masters are still the Negro
faith.

Southerners cherish to the highest degree a great American
superstition: that the school is a social panacea. If the unsus-
pecting stranger studies the plans of the section's schools, he
may conclude that the purpose of these institutions is not only

to make Southern youths into Northerners but also to make
them into communists of the variety Plato describes in *The
Republic*. Textbooks written in the North give an anti-South-
ern bias to instruction in history, literature, and speech, and
the school seemingly is attempting to usurp many of the
functions of child nurture traditionally belonging to the
home.

But among Southerners there is the education which does
not educate. This result is caused partly by the temperament
of a people inclined to be leisurely and even Philistine. It is
caused also by the survival of overwhelming traditions. Northern bias in textbooks is offset by less formal and perhaps more
effective indoctrination in local ideals which survive the regimentation of the schools. Many Northern teachers in Southern schools feel obligated, not always reluctantly, to acquire
the regional bias. The home, not the school, determines the
cultural outlook of Southerners. It is remarkable how seldom
the problems raised in the classroom are discussed in the
market place or around the dinner table; how perfect is the
freedom of speech enjoyed by the teacher because few bother
to repeat the teacher's opinions; and how unused is the public
to listen to the collective opinions of teachers or students; and
how even lessons in a subject so "scientific" as cooking have
difficulty in changing the home diet. How little the college
affects its surroundings is revealed by the fact that the volun-
tary reading habits of the college community are nearly the
same as those of the nonacademic community. Proof of this
comes from the comparison of the books and magazines sold
in corner drug stores.

The South accepts Northern dictation in literary matters
more completely than in other fields. A book, even one about
the South and by a Southerner, wins little attention from

Southerners unless published in New York. In order to win
the approval of New York, the Southern author sometimes
feels obligated to use a critical realism, or romantic irony
which involves a ridicule of the Southern past. Many among
educated Southerners commit a major crime against intelligence; instead of letting their opinions of state or section grow
out of their own observations, they accept the opinions of
New York journalists as paraphrased for them by their local
newspapers.

There is danger, however, of overemphasizing literary materials in measuring the outlook of a people as nonliterary as
those of the South. Most Southern readers ignore the realistic
writings, nourishing themselves on the self-flattery of historical romance. Many among the minority who read the new
realism do not connect it with life, regarding it as a vicarious
escape into a sentimental world which they do not actually
wish to enter. Moreover, the new school of Southern writers
belongs to the South to a greater degree than earlier critics
realized. This was expressed in the continued success of *Gone
With the Wind,* an obvious glorification of the Old South. It
is now realized that behind the stinking vulgarity of Erskine
Caldwell lies a lusty and even humorous appreciation of the
Southern poor white; that behind the seemingly unreasoning
violence of William Faulkner lies a legend of the South as
patriotic as it is pessimistic; that James Branch Cabell, despite
his irreverence, is able to move among medieval legends with
a sense of continuity with aristocratic Virginia; and that Ellen
Glasgow, despite her bleak landscapes and progressive hopes,
has compassion for her unprogressive Virginians.

Forces work against the apparent progress from rural stag-
nation to urbanization. Southerners who move from country
to city and factory do not surrender their rural ideals. In the

South the country conquers the city as effectively as elsewhere the city conquers the country. The larger Southern cities grow, the less do they become cities in the cultural sense; unlike the cities of Europe and the North, they do not emphasize such urban arts as the theater, the drama, and music; nor do they have good cooking in public places. This is because a larger and larger proportion of their inhabitants possess rural backgrounds and are naturally most interested in country pleasures. The wealthy of the new Southern cities spend their surpluses on farms, country estates, horses, hogs, hunting, and city houses in country style.

The march toward America's ideal of democracy is stayed that the splendid legend of the Old South might be preserved. "Perpetually suspended in the great haze of memory," according to Cash, "it hung, as it were, poised, somewhere between earth and sky, colossal, shining, and incomparably lovely." The attitude of the old agrarian aristocracy continued to be a part of the Southern tradition, not only in the thirty-five years after 1865 but also into the twentieth century. Everyone who claimed to be a planter was metamorphosed into a Marse Chan or a Squire Effingham. "The Southerner feels," wrote William Van Conner in 1948, "that the ante-bellum world possessed values and a way-of-life in which the needs of the whole human being could be more readily satisfied than they could be in our industrialized society."

Ancestor-hunting is an important activity. Many persons tie themselves to baronial planters and some—if we accept the word of James Branch Cabell and Stark Young—trace descent from the Ten Lost Tribes of Israel. Such an attitude tends to create an atrophying pessimism; an incomplete and frustrated region, as William Faulkner puts it, a region vainly trying to recover its identity, vainly trying to relive its legendary past. This attitude also possesses constructive social functions. A consciousness of illustrious forebears gives satisfactions not unlike those of religion to old people without material assets. It gives justifications to the ambitions or attainments of self-made men, freeing them of inferiority complexes and getting them into the best society. It gives rise to the cult of antique furniture, the reproduction of which is the most appreciated thing of beauty the twentieth-century South produces.

The changing South of the legend works both ways. Changes in the direction of national uniformity are accompanied by changes in the opposite direction. Important among the latter is the disappearance of the fear of the hot climate inherited from European ancestors. This is because of the invention of artificial ice and of refrigeration and because of the elimination of such climatic evils as malaria, yellow fever, and hookworm. The habiliments of the ancestors have been replaced by looser and lighter garments. The Victorian modesty of the maiden has been replaced by a nakedness almost as complete as that of a pagan goddess. The South has learned to regard the sun as a beneficent god instead of a cruel tyrant. Its curative properties are now regarded as a protection for rural Southerners against lack of sanitary devices. Sun baths are indulged in for two reasons: because of health and because of an aesthetic revolution which holds that a brown skin is more beautiful than a fair one. The acme of Southern comeliness is blue eyes, blond hair, and bronze skin.

Many of the regional characteristics herewith listed are survivals out of a dark past and are persistently condemned by outsiders. If they are defended by Southerners, it is with fundamental qualifications. The South of the twentieth century has no intention of declaring "a positive good" those aspects

of its behavior which affront the national majority. It, however, finds it not only possible but practically wise to defend
as "positively good" certain of its peculiar ambitions and tendencies. There are certain developments which, unlike those
behind the proslavery argument of the Old South, do not run
counter to the liberal sentiments of the outside world. The
South, long accused of tyranny against others, can, with a
show of reason, accuse others of tyranny against it.

"Positively good" is the demand that the section be allowed
to adjust its artistic expressions to the climate and temperament of its people. Because of the tyranny of books and magazines imported from strange climates, Southerners are
prompted to construct artificial lakes, treeless lawns, and low-
roofed houses without porches or blinds. These lakes are often
mosquito-infested and slimy or muddy; the lawns are often
bare and unkempt; and the houses are often uncomfortably
hot for six months of the year. Southern suburbs often possess
the chaotic appearance of a parade of circus cages. The newer
public monuments sometimes stress the sensational and the
realistic. Comfort and inherited taste demand a return to the
tangled garden, to shade-giving trees, to the porches and high-
roofed halls of ante-bellum homes, and to public monuments
in which the classical ideals of the section are respected.
Southerners have as much right to their peculiarities as do
other peoples.

One of the prices the South pays for its progressive industrialization is increasing servitude to Northern capital. New
York has grown into the most autocratic city-state of modern
times, with the Southern province of the United States as one
of its important colonies. The great financial houses of that
and kindred cities control most of the region's strategic industries, having sent out a second and third generation of

carpetbaggers to found factories or to purchase those already existing. The Southern industries owned and controlled by outsiders include the region's railroads, its coal fields, its iron reserves, its electric power, and its gas, sulphur, and oil resources. The existence of Northern patent monopolies and the absence of local machine manufacturing permit outside direction even of industries locally owned. Manufacturing was until the middle of the twentieth century confined mainly to the elementary processes. The South fabricates its own cast-iron pipes, steel rails, bridges, and oils; but not its hardware, locomotives, automobiles, clocks, radios, dynamos, drugs, and many other finished products requiring the highest skill to produce and bringing in the highest profits.

Retail profits are siphoned out of the section by Northern-owned chain stores. Only a few of the "specialty" articles made excessively profitable through national advertising are controlled by Southerners. The Southern businessman usually is a mere factor or agent of Northern principals, who control both production and distribution. His function is to sell the gasoline, automobiles, mechanical refrigerators, alcoholic beverages, clothing, insurance policies, and a hundred other articles endeared to the Southern public through advertising. Some of these articles are as worthless as the wooden nutmegs the Yankee peddler is said to have imposed upon the public in ante-bellum days. The burden of these purchases on a relatively poor people is injurious. In 1937 economist David Coyle estimated that the South was paying out a billion dollars annually in excess of its income. It balanced its credit by selling property to investors from other sections of the country, by borrowing, by going bankrupt, and by destroying forests and lands to secure immediate incomes.

Apparently there is no effective remedy for this situation.

The Federal government, through its policies of protective tariffs, constitutional immunities to corporations, railroad rate discriminations, and patent monopolies, customarily favors the older manufacturing centers of the country. The possibility of the South's revolting against its debtor status, in the manner of the Revolutionary planters against their British creditors, is ruled out by the outcome of the Civil War. That Southern leaders are able to reconcile the sons and grandsons of those who followed Robert E. Lee and William Jennings Bryan to the economic domination of the North caused Benjamin Kendrick to cry out bitterly in 1942: "We are confronted with a paradox more amazing and ironical than any ever conjured by the imagination of Gilbert and Sullivan. The people of the South, who all their lives have suffered deprivation, want, and humiliation from an outside finance imperialism, followed with hardly a murmur of protest leaders who, if indirectly, were nonetheless agents and attorneys of the imperialists." What was true in 1942 is truer thirty years later.

However, there are protests which excite the moral sympathies of those liberals the world over who condemn colonial exploitation. William Faulkner may be creating in his hideous character Popeye a compendium of the rape and corruption which alien finance capitalism visits upon the novelist's homeland. Academicians like Walter P. Webb of Texas and Howard W. Odum of North Carolina furnished the facts concerning the South's plight; President Franklin D. Roosevelt's National Emergency Council broadcasted these facts.

Some economists regard the Roosevelt-Kennedy policy of heavy expenditures of the Federal government a means of lessening the annual excess of capitalistic enterprise imposed upon the South. It is believed that the levying of huge Federal

income taxes according to ability to pay, and the expenditure
of these revenues according to the degree of human need,
meant a shift of resources from the wealthier North to the
poorer South. The Federal expenditures of the period of
World War II and its aftermath created an unparalleled prosperity which has resulted in a greater proportional increase in
Southern incomes and allowed Southerners to retire a considerable portion of their debts. Southern ports like Hampton
Roads and New Orleans impinge upon the commercial mo-
nopoly of New York City. The partial victory against freight-
rate discriminations presaged a reversal of long-established
Federal policies of favoritism to patrons of Northern carriers.
The Tennessee Valley development is a magnificent gesture
by the Federal government toward redressing the grievances
of the South against the rapacity of the financiers who captured the section's electric power. The success of this experiment may lead to its duplication in other areas as an additional means of redressing the balance against the Southern
and other regional economies.

Under the direction of Southern entrepreneurs one great
Southern industry annexed the whole United States as its
province. This is tobacco under the direction of the Dukes
and the Reynoldses. Other comparable successes are Coca-
Cola and patent medicines. The South's most mature industry, cotton textiles, has learned to make fabrics of the finest
quality, and under the trade names of Cannon, Dan River
and Avondale is capturing profitable national markets. These
may be followed by triumphs in other fields; Southern labor
is growing more skilled and Southern business more cunning.
The workingman is astir with the obvious intention of exacting the highest possible wages from employers, be they local
or Northern. The Southern farmer is giving up his traditional

conservatism to form trade agreements and crop-reduction compacts to exact the highest prices from Northern consumers.

Perhaps the greatest threat to the integrity of the regional life is that the South will succumb to bribes offered by the wealthier section of the country. There is precedent for such behavior. Robert E. Lee's refusal to accept a sinecure from a Northern business concern did not prevent other former Confederate generals from doing so. The Reconstruction period was scarcely over before these men and other leaders of Southern opinion took action which had the earmarks of scalawagism. Northern business leaders invaded every Southern state, offering the gospel of prosperity. They invited the local leaders to what one historian has picturesquely called the Great Barbecue. These leaders, with a few exceptions, took their places at the table in order to participate in the profits of the new business. They became the agents or hired attorneys of the invading capitalists. The Great Barbecue continues to the present, with the table growing longer and longer to make room for a greater variety of Southern leaders. The hospitality grows so generous that a Georgia writer, Calvin Kytle, believes that both sides in the struggle for the control of state affairs receive financial support from the capitalists. The Kennedy administration through Federal subsidies to public schools may induce a growing number of Southern communities to abandon segregation.

Southern educators receive subsidies from the capitalistic philanthropies of the North for the purpose of carrying on research which, at least by implication, discredits the traditional race and social distinctions of the South. Inherited concepts of States' Rights are set aside in order that Southern politicians, businessmen, farmers, and commoners may share

in the ever increasing Federal bounties. Donald Davidson
thinks that under the reforming zeal of Federal social plan-
ners the Tennessee Valley may become a region of forests,
pastures, and lakes in which the once busy grower of tobacco
or cotton will be "a tipped purveyor and a professional friend
to tippling fishermen."

That the South is willing to sacrifice moral and even religious scruples for the proverbial mess of potage is illustrated
by the repeal of prohibition. A five-decade battle against
Demon Rum culminated in every Southern state giving its
consent to the Eighteenth Amendment. Some who felt that
they knew the region well believed that prohibition had become the Eleventh Commandment, a fruition of the Southern
combination of puritanism and reticence. The unexpected
happened. All the Southern states except Mississippi repealed
prohibition. A New York dominated national administration
wanted the revival of the liquor industry as a means of escap-
ing the Great Depression of 1929. Revenue-hungry Southern
politicians saw in the revived liquor traffic a rich source of
income. The South Carolina legislature, half-repentant over
its violation of a righteous heritage, re-enacted prohibition on
condition that substitute revenues be found for the inevitable
losses. No substitutes were found, and South Carolina continued wet.

"I wish," said a Georgia professor recently, "that Miss Mil-
lie would come back to life and drive the rascals out with her
broomstick." He was referring to Mildred D. Rutherford, a
publicist who defended the South by sharp attacks on Northerners, and on the imported critics of Southern ways in Southern universities who created a feeling of inferiority among
Southern youths. These critics make comparisons between the
region's creature comforts and those of the rest of the nation:

the comparative scarcity in the South of house paint, plumbing, hospital beds, individual wealth, balanced diets, neat lawns and barns, magazine and newspaper readers, and the thousand and one conveniences and tricks which are more plentiful in the North. The critics have established the legend of a gully-washed land inhabited by a lazy and contented people.

The South has listened to these criticisms and derived much benefit from them. It does not wish to experience again the privations of the 1860's, when an attempted revolution cut its communications with the more progressive section of the United States. At the same time, thoughtful Southerners feel that there is room for intelligent criticisms of the complaints of outsiders. Perhaps many current adverse comments on the South are mere repetitions of British travelers' condemnations, a hundred years ago, of Kentucky for being shabbier and poorer than neat and very rich Ohio. Such criticism is as unintelligent as condemning a citizen of a town as a wastrel because he is not so rich as his richest neighbor. That the South today is not so richly endowed with wealth and creature comforts as the rest of the richest country on earth does not prove that the region below the Potomac is poor and unprogressive. This region, indeed, is fabulously rich compared with the neighboring countries of Central and South America, richer than any large area of the world outside the United States.

It is time to be philosophical about the comparative backwardness of the South. History and geography explain it in part. An additional explanation is that the people of the section, in the interest of worldly ease or Christian ideals, prefer contentment to chasing after material values which do not lead to paradise. "In taking on work," says Norman Foerster, a discerning student of the sectional differences, "the new South has not forgotten everything else." The Southerner's conception of wisdom is usually not gratified by spending his idle moments keeping his house and garden perfectly neat, as many Northerners do; his sense of values calls for recreations, even dissipations, at the expense of physical perfections. The self-respecting Southerner, unlike the self-respecting Northerner, is not absorbed by the need of saving for old age. If the worst comes, the Southerner can achieve social security at the expense of usually willing relatives or a benevolent government.

Recent American history is characterized by renewed challenges to the principle of regional self-determination. Political parties, vying for leadership in what Americans call democracy, are again demanding the blotting out of many of the South's racial distinctions. The South is able to strike back with a good chance of being able to maintain its traditional position. It feels that the Constitution of the United States, if not the Federal courts, is on its side in matters of intimate concern. It believes that America is not ready to become a consolidated democracy at the expense of the Federal Republic. It believes that it possesses the right to deal with the blacks within the limits of the national conscience; that its liberal apologists and critics are correct in asserting that it is making progress in ironing out race discriminations; and that its violations of democratic concepts in respect to the blacks are in reality not much worse than what takes place in the North. The good Southerner is constantly discovering cases of ill treatment of Negroes in such places as Detroit, Harlem, and Chicago.

The pressures in favor of national standardization have been great and the surrenders numerous. Social critic Robert

Heilman finds in the South "a sheer love of the up-to-date," a conscious going "after streamlined industrialization that is elsewhere not so expressly planned," and "a triumphant 'progressive' education which progresses even faster than in the North and which has been rushing school systems off into a life of sin as fast as they are born." Nevertheless, the South is proud of the fact that for 100 years it has been able to couple an unsuspected loyalty to the nation with customs and folkways which vary most from the national monotony pictured by Sinclair Lewis. The region below the Potomac retains its own manners, its own speech, its own temperament, and the multitude of subtle peculiarities by reason of which the uniformity of the section with the nation turns out to be more a physical than a psychological reality. The Southern people, claimed Foerster after a ten years' absence from North Carolina, "impress one at once with their different voices, different accent, their sense of manners, the courtesy which appears in all classes, their organic folksiness (as if of one family), their awareness of the past as a force both hampering and helping."

FOUR

NEW VIEWPOINTS OF
SOUTHERN RECONSTRUCTION

THE issues of most periods of American history have been
so satisfactorily settled that they are now significant only
as possible explanations of aspects of contemporary events
and institutions. This is not true of the main issue of the Reconstruction period: the race question. It is almost as timely
today as when it arose in 1865; as one of its prominent students says, like Banquo's ghost it will not down. Conse-
quently, interpretations of the ten or twelve years following
the Civil War seem destined, for an indefinite period, to have
an influence beyond mere explanations of past events. The
successful historian of Reconstruction, by revealing early
phases of the still burning race question, arouses more attention among the reading public than is usually accorded historical works.

This continued survival of the leading issue of the post-
bellum era explains why the interpretations of those years are
so varied and numerous. Conservative scholars have described
the follies and rascalities of Negro politicians and their Car-

petbagger friends so as to make the reader thankful that such knavery cannot be repeated in his time. Less scrupulous writers have so effectively correlated the events of Reconstruction with those of their own times that their books have been best sellers. The outstanding example of this is Claude Bowers' *Tragic Era,* in which an attack upon the Republican enemies of Alfred E. Smith in 1928 is veiled behind attacks upon the Republican leaders of 1868, 1872, and 1876. At least one novelist has so effectively connected certain lurid aspects of Reconstruction with the race prejudices prevailing in the South in his times that the situations he described have become a part of the Southern folk beliefs. The Ku Klux Klan is used as either a glamorous or sinister symbol to arouse issues of race, religion, and patriotism in which all Americans, radicals and reactionaries, Negro lovers and Negro haters, are vitally and perennially concerned. Reconstruction does not escape the attention of contemporary religionists; and even the Marxians, who would settle great social and economic issues, use Reconstruction experiences in their arguments.

A biased interpretation of Reconstruction caused one of the most important political developments in the recent history of the South, the disfranchisement of the blacks. The fraud and violence by which this objective was first obtained was justified on a single ground: the memory of the alleged horrors of Reconstruction. Later, amid a flood of oratory concerned with this memory, the white rulers of the South, in constitutional conventions of the 1890's and 1900's, devised legal means to eliminate the Negro vote. "Reconstruction," asserted the prime justifier of this act, "was this villainy, anarchy, misrule and robbery, and I cannot, in any words that I possess, paint it." These words of Ben Tillman were endorsed by all shades of white opinion from Carter Glass, Henry W.

Grady, and Charles B. Aycock to Tom Watson, Hoke Smith, and James K. Vardaman.

Historians, sensing that the discrediting of the period in which the Negro most freely participated in politics justifies his subsequent exclusion from those activities, have condemned Reconstruction measures as sweepingly as have the Southern politicians. They have called the military rule by which these measures were inaugurated "as brutish a tyranny as ever marked the course of any government whose agents and organs claimed to be civilized"; they have termed the best of the Carpetbaggers "infamous scoundrels"; and they have described the enfranchised freedmen as belonging to a race "incapable of forming any judgment upon the actions of men." The article on South Carolina in the eleventh edition of the *Encyclopedia Britannica* in all seriousness concludes: "All the misfortunes of war itself are insignificant when compared with the sufferings of the people during Reconstruction."

In midcentury the masses of white Southerners accepted these judgments as axiomatic. White Southerners would argue the issues of the Civil War and even the merits of the Democratic party, but there was scarcely one in a position of authority who would debate Negro suffrage and the related issues of Reconstruction. The wickedness of this régime and the righteousness of the manner in which it was destroyed were fundamentals of his civic code. Such a condemnation or commendation justifies the settlement of questions of the immediate past and are invoked to settle issues of even the remote future.

This extremely partisan judgment of still timely historical events imposes upon the historian of Reconstruction a serious civic duty. He must foster more moderate, saner, perhaps newer views of his period in the light of his investigations of the processes of Reconstruction.

The capital blunder of the chronicler of Reconstruction is to treat that period like Carlyle's portrayal of the French Revolution, as a melodrama involving wild-eyed conspirators whose acts are best described in red flashes upon a canvas. Such a treatment creates the impression that Southern society was frenzied by misery. This is at best the picturesque pageantry of the artist; at worst, the cheap sensationalism of the journalist or the scenario writer. At all odds it is woefully one-sided and unhistorical. Of course the South during Reconstruction, like France during the Revolution, had its prophets of despair, its fanatical idealists, its unprincipled knaves. Luckily the behavior of these damned souls is not the whole story of Reconstruction, but merely a partial recording of the political aspects of the era. Some of the political acts were as sane and constructive as those of the French Revolution. They were concerned with educational, constitutional, and political reform, and were instrumental in putting the Southern states in line with the progressive spirit of the nineteenth century.

The aberrations of the Reconstruction politicians were not accurate barometers of the actual behavior of the Southern people. The Reconstruction governments were not natural developments from the conditions inherent in Southern life, but were, in a sense, artificial impositions from without. Frenzied politics did not necessarily reflect a frenzied social life. Despite strange doings in statehouses, the Southern people of both races lived as quietly and as normally during Reconstruction as in any politically disturbed period before or after. The defiance of the traditional caste division occasionally expressed in an official reception or in an act of the

legislature was not reflected generally in common social relations. No attempt was made to destroy white supremacy
in the social or economic sphere or to sanction interracial
marriages. The political aggressiveness of the Negroes, char-
acteristic of the period, did not extend to other phases of human relations. A staunch Republican voter was often a good
servant in the house of a white Democrat. Negro officeholders
who were aggressive politically were known to observe care-
fully the etiquette of the Southern caste system.

Moreover, in aspects of life not directly political there were
achievements during the post-bellum era so quietly constructive that they have escaped the attention of most historians.
This is true even of Du Bois, the Negro author who ardently
and extensively defends the Reconstruction record of his race.

Foremost among these achievements were agricultural reforms. While official agencies through Black Codes and the
Freedmen's Bureau were making fragmentary and generally
unsuccessful attempts to redefine a shattered rural economy,
the freedmen bargained themselves into an agricultural situation unlike that of slavery and from their viewpoint advan-
tageous. They worked beyond official purview. Although
they were unable to gain legal title to the lands, they forced
white competitors, for their labor in the expanding cotton
fields, to establish them on separate farms in houses scattered
over the land. This abandonment of the communal character
of the Southern plantation bestowed upon Negroes the American farmer's ideal of independent existence. This was a revolutionary reform more important in the actual life of freedmen than the sensational but largely unsuccessful political
changes attempted at the time. The share crop agreements
and other types of labor contracts between the freedmen and
the landlords soon became fixed by custom.

Changes scarcely less significant took place in the religious sphere. Under slavery autonomous Negro churches had not been tolerated and blacks were forced to attend churches directed both administratively and doctrinally by the master race. During Reconstruction the freedmen successfully asserted religious freedom and established independent churches. This secession was accomplished with a minimum of ill feeling and without important doctrinal or ritualistic innovations by the seceding groups. But it was a momentous change in social relations. It has been permanent, having never been challenged by even the most reactionary social forces. It is important to a people so intensely religious as are Southerners of both races. The existence of perfectly independent Negro churches has given the black race opportunity for self-expression studiously denied it since Reconstruction in political and other nonreligious fields.

Another radical but constructive change of a nonpolitical character was the development of a new commercial system. The breakup of the plantations into small units created much small trade and a consequent demand for small credit. This was met by the creation of the crossroads stores and the commercial villages and towns with stores and banks. These new institutions were owned by an emergent economic group, the storekeepers, who dominated the Southern community as effectively, if not as glamorously, as the planters had once done. The storekeepers were often also bankers, planters, church deacons, and sometimes state senators. Their power was based on large profits realized from the new system of credit advances on unharvested crops.

The assertion that the abnormalities of post-bellum politics did not adequately reflect the actualities of Southern life leads to the conviction that a balanced understanding of the period

cannot be had without descriptions of social life. The social
activities of both races remained relatively wholesome and
happy; there was little of the misery, hatred, and repression
often sweepingly ascribed to it by writers. There were camp
meetings, dances, balls, tournaments, picnics, parades, agricultural fairs, lavish banquets, and indulgence in the vanities
of personal adornment. There was, of course, much poverty,
the shadow of the Lost Cause, and apprehension concerning
possible events in the political world. But there were fresh
memories of heroic events, and there were surviving warriors
to give glamorous reality to these memories. Gaiety was dis-
ciplined by recent tragedy, but it was not dampened by the
utilitarianism of a more progressive age.

The claim that the times were completely dominated by
stark pessimism is refuted by the fact that during Reconstruction the optimistic concept called the New South was born.
It is true that predictions concerning a new civilization
springing from the ruins of slavery and the Confederacy were
premature. It was ridiculous to call newspapers established
amid the ruins of Columbia and the rice plantations *The
Phoenix* and *The New South*. But the spirit of progress
abroad in the land was not stifled by varied difficulties. It was
fostered by some hopeful actualities—a new commercial life,
the new banks, the high price of cotton, and the new agriculture made possible by the first extensive use of commercial
fertilizer. These were not the "good old days," but an optimistic note was reflected in the newspapers. When in the
1880's this hopefulness germinated in the actualities of new
industries and a philosophy of progress and reconciliation, it
was from the seeds sown in the two previous decades.

In one sense, those who have essayed books on Reconstruction have closed their narratives before the actual reconstruc-

tion in the South began. The Northern reformers who arrived in the 1860's and 1870's carrying carpetbags were driven out by Southerners armed with shotguns before these outsiders could make their projects effective. But a later generation of Northern reformers, coming mostly in the twentieth century, have experienced a different reception. Riding in expensive automobiles, emanating an aura of wealth, this later generation has, through lavish expenditures, received the enthusiastic co-operation of Southerners. They have introduced Northern ideals of literature, architecture, and landscaping, and have instilled into the Southern mind a definite preference for Northern concepts of civilization.

Those of us who are not willing to accept this thesis that the true reconstruction did not come until years after the so-called Reconstruction, should nevertheless feel obligated to watch for evidence during the 1870's of the beginnings of the industrial, cultural, and psychical conquest by the North of the South which has shown itself so clearly in recent decades. Perhaps hidden beneath the seemingly premature and erratic actions of the Carpetbaggers were plans which have been executed by the rich Northerners of the twentieth century.

As has been suggested, one of the most striking features of Southern society is the color line. This division under slavery was not as sharp as it is today. The influences of Reconstruction induced this sharpening. The aggressiveness of the blacks and their allies caused resentment among the whites and consequent estrangement between the races. This alienation in turn caused the blacks, especially in social and economic relations, to grow more independent. If this thesis is true, the careful student of the post-bellum period is obligated to isolate those interests and attitudes which account for the intensification of the caste division of Southern society. In doing this he will perhaps help explain the most important reality of interracial relations.

One of the accepted conventions of Reconstruction scholars is that the Carpetbaggers failed because their measures were excessively radical. We have often been told how the Four Million were suddenly hurled from slavery into freedom; how black barbarians were forced to attempt the roles of New England gentlemen; how seven hundred thousand of these illiterates were given the vote and the privilege of officehold-ing. But were these measures genuine radicalism, actual up-rootings which inevitably led to fundamental changes in Southern society? The answer is that they were scarcely more than artificial or superimposed remedies from the outside which in no real sense struck at the roots of Southern life.

A truly radical program would have called for the con-fiscation of land for the freedmen. Land was the principal form of Southern wealth, the only effective weapon with which the ex-slaves could have battled for economic com-petence and social equality. But the efforts of the Freedmen's Bureau in the direction of land endowments for its wards were fitful and abortive. Conservative constitutional theory opposed any such meaningful enfranchisement. The domi-nant Radicalism of the day naïvely assumed that a people's salvation could be obtained through the ballot and the spell-ing book. The freedmen got these but were allowed to con-tinue in physical want, and even lost the industrial skills and disciplines they had inherited from slavery. No wonder they carried bags in which to bear away their suffrage and ex-pected education to place them at the tables of the rich and competent. They were realists, and their so-called benefactors were the deluded ones. Wise Tory statesmen like Bismarck, Lord Salisbury, and Alexander II would have put something in their bags and endowed them with tangible social privilege.

In another vital respect the so-called Radicals of the 1860's lost an opportunity to attempt genuine radicalism. They did not try to destroy the greatest obstacle to the Negroes' salvation, the Southern caste system. Contemporary professions of such attempts lack sincerity. Anglo-Saxon race pride, New England standards of civilization, a respect for narrowly Protestant standards of morality were in the way. Attempts at fraternization between the races were stilted official affairs lacking that unconscious informality on which true sociability must be based. No one was ever allowed to forget that race distinctions existed.

A distinguished Negro lecturer recently stated that the whole truth is not told by those books which assert that the blacks and their coadjutors were the sole aggressors of the Reconstruction period. Revolution was attempted on both sides. The blacks, of course, on their part, were sufficiently aggressive to demand the continuation of freedom and the vote and the liberties implied in these terms. But the whites also showed an aggressiveness which went beyond the maintenance of their traditional position in Southern society. They tightened the bonds of caste; they deprived the subordinate caste of many occupational opportunities enjoyed under slavery; they drove colored farmers from the land; they gradually deprived the blacks of a well-integrated position and imposed on them a status akin to pariahs whom many wished exiled. The disappearance of aristocratic prejudices against many forms of honest labor created the conviction that it was possible for Southern society to function without the despised African. Certainly an appraisal of the helplessness of the blacks at the close of the Reconstruction era makes one wonder why the whites are not more often adjudged the actual revolutionaries of the times. Victory was in white hands—the actuality as well as the sentiment and the tradition.

Several generations of historians have asserted that the Reconstruction governments were so grievously corrupt and extravagant that they checked all efforts at material rehabilitation. There was, of course, corruption and waste—expensive spittoons, thousand dollar bribes, fraudulent bonds, and so on. But the actual financial burdens of government which tolerated such acts have been exaggerated. Their expenditures seem small when compared with the budgets of twentieth-century states and extravagant only against the parsimony of the governments immediately preceding and following. The extravagant bond issues of the Reconstruction governments were not an immediate burden upon contemporaries, and afflicted subsequent generations only to the extent to which they were not repudiated. The Radical governments, like the government of Louis XVI in France, failed not because their expenditures were burdensome but because they did not enjoy enough power and respect to force the taxpayers to yield funds sufficient to discharge the obligations of effective political establishments. There was a taxpayers' strike rather than a tax collectors' orgy. Some Reconstruction governments could not pay their gas bills.

A reinterpretation of the tax policies of the Radical régimes suggests a new explanation of the odius reputations possessed by these governments. Of course, a partial answer is that there was corruption and incompetence. Illiterate freedmen were easily seduced by scalawags and unscrupulous Carpetbaggers. But were these malpractices the most serious offenses of the Reconstructionists? It seems that the worst crime of which they have been adjudged guilty was the violation of the American caste system. The crime of crimes was to encourage Negroes in voting, officeholding, and other functions of social equality. This supposedly criminal encouragement of the Negro is execrated ever more savagely as with the passing years race prejudices continue to mount. Mild-mannered historians declare that the assertiveness resulting therefrom was grotesque and abnormal, while the more vehement writers call it the worst of civic scandals. Attempts to make the Reconstruction governments reputable and honest have been treated with scorn, and the efforts of Negroes to approach the white man's standards of civilization are adjudged more reprehensible than the behavior of the more ignorant and corrupt. Social equality and negroism have not a chance to be respectable.

Such views logically grow out of the conviction that the Negro belongs to an innately inferior race and is therefore incapable by his very nature of exercising with sagacity the higher attributes of civilization. James Ford Rhodes gives the viewpoint of moderate historians by declaring the Negro to be "one of the most inferior races of mankind" and by endorsing Brinton's theory of the Negro's arrested development at adolescence. John W. Burgess voices the opinions of the more prejudiced when he says: "The claim that there is nothing in the color of the skin is a great sophism. A black skin means membership in a race of men which has never succeeded in subjecting passion to reason." Less critical writers take such statements to be so obviously true that they need no specific affirmation.

The impartial historian, however, cannot so readily endorse this finding. His knowledge of the conclusions of modern anthropology casts grave doubts on the innate inferiority of the blacks. This knowledge, indeed, creates the necessity of explaining the conduct of the Negroes, during Reconstruction as well as during other times, on other than racial grounds. It also leads to the rejection of the gloomy generalization that the race, because of its inherent nature, is destined to play forever its present inferior role.

Loose assertions concerning Reconstruction as an attempt to return to the ideals of the jungle, as an effort to rebarbarize the Negro and to make South Carolina and Mississippi into African provinces, seem to have no basis in truth. Indeed, the exact opposite seems nearer the truth. Reconstruction can be interpreted as a definite step forward in the Anglicization or the Americanization of the blacks, certainly not their Africanization. The sagacious William A. Dunning tells the truth when he asserts that the newly-liberated freedmen were "fascinated with the pursuit of the white man's culture." This passion did not abate during the later years of Reconstruction; it is still a dominant feature of Negro life. The zeal with which the ex-slaves sought the benefits of literary education is unparalleled in history; this was the most obvious means of assimilating the white man's culture. Although Negro society during the first years of freedom tended to grow independent of white society, it continued to imitate the culture of the superior caste. Among the more cultivated Negroes, the more independent their society is of the whites', the stronger the resemblance. The radical changes in Negro religion which grew out of freedom were not in the direction of Africa, but rather in the direction of frontier or backwoods America, with some imitations of Fifth Avenue standards of clerical correctness. The misbehavior of Negro politicians had no African coloring. Their bad manners were those of American rustics and their vices were not unlike those of contemporary Tammany politicians. It is true that variations in the dialect of the Southern Negroes were most pronounced in the years after the war, or at least they were then best recognized; but even in the Gullah speech of the Sea Islands, African words did not predominate.

The efforts of certain Negroes of the post-bellum period to establish African connections were abortive. When cultured Negroes like Martin R. Dulany tried to discover their African ancestors, they were guilty of a fatuous Americanism, different only in one respect from that of Americans who trace their ancestors in England: the African quest could not be successful. The influences of slavery had resulted in such a thorough Americanization of the blacks that little African was left in their culture. This was the main reason why the efforts during Reconstruction to promote emigration to Liberia were a dismal failure. There was no more cultural affinity between the Southern Negro and his African blood kin than between the American Negro and the Chinese.

The aspersions on the freedmen for emulating the white man's culture have been as unfair as the criticisms of them for the alleged attempt to Africanize the South. Numerous writers have ridiculed sooty women for wearing veils and gloves, for carrying umbrellas, for calling themselves "Mrs." and "Miss," and for retiring from the fields to establish firesides and homes. Likewise, the spectacle of Negro politicians trying to talk like Daniel Webster or Charles Sumner has caused jest, and undue emphasis has been placed upon the impracticability of the attempt to load the curricula of Negro schools with items of classical culture adapted from New England. But are these criticisms just? It is granted that such aspirations after the white man's culture were often the result of uncritical enthusiasms and were beyond the immediate reach of an inexperienced people turned loose naked in the world. But measured according to the unescapable standards of American civilization, were these aspirations in the wrong direction? Were they not in the direction all Americans, including even those relegated to the lowest caste, seek to travel? The major problem of the American Negro is to attain the standards of American civilization. This is a decree of circumstances which the American Negro has accepted without reluctance. Therefore, the Reconstructionists who held Boston and Massachusetts up as ideals for the blacks were not giving the wrong advice. The fact that this advice moved the Negroes profoundly, if not always sagaciously, is a tribute to the sound instincts of these blacks and of their Reconstruction mentors.

Historians of the South should adopt a more critical, creative, and tolerant attitude toward so important a period in the annals of their section as Reconstruction. This will promote truth and scholarship in the austere sense of those terms. It will do more. It will banish that provincialism which is based on priggishness and ignorance of comparisons; it will fortify the sound provincialism born of better understanding of one's own province; and it will enrich those measured evaluations which are possible only after contact with other people's provinces. A better comprehension of the Reconstruction past will aid in the solution of the South's great race problem. Bias and passion should be explained in rational terms in order that contemporaries may better understand the forces motivating them. In this modest way the great civic obligation of the historian can be discharged.

FIVE

THE RISING TIDE OF FAITH

FAITH in the Biblical heritage is a factor second only to White Supremacy as a means of conserving the ways of the South. The historians often say revolutionary changes that enveloped the European continent in the last few centuries stopped with the Pyrenees. Historians of the United States say with equal reason that revolutionary changes in this country stop with the Potomac. Spain and the South have remained conservative because of the unrelenting piety of Spanish and Southern peoples.

The hold of orthodox Protestantism upon Southerners of the twentieth century is a likely explanation of why the section, in the face of earth-shaking changes in industry, transportation, and education, has kept its identity as the most conservative portion of the United States. Fundamental convictions in matters of faith account for the difficulty of arousing Southern churches to the need of social reform and for the indifference of Southerners to nonreligious agitations except those of a political or purely practical nature. Public forums, even in large cities, are rare, and soapbox orators of the Hyde Park or Union Square variety discoursing on other than religious subjects are unknown. Faith, to expand Karl Marx's adage, is in the South the opiate of the rich as well as the poor. A Southern journalist moving to the secular atmosphere of a Northern university despairingly remarks that the pervading influence of orthodoxy had recreated an Old South unable to grow into a New South.

The modern South has made progress in technology and education, the handmaidens of faith. The growing cities of Nashville and Memphis blaze with the latest neon signs beckoning people to attend the fundamentalist adjurations of the Church of Christ. The radios of the Piedmont textile belt echo with warnings of Holy Roller preachers—even with utterance in Unknown Tongues. Manger scenes appear during the Christmas season in front of churches stretching from the Rio Grande to the Potomac with an extravagance impossible before the time of spotlights and plastics.

The implementation of universal education by the Southern States bids fair to be the means of making Christianity universal. This may happen despite a decree of the United States Supreme Court attempting to restrict the teaching of religion in schools. Educational institutions all over the South resound with daily prayers, hymns, and Bible reading; early in December the school children begin the decoration of their classrooms in preparation for the coming of the Christ Child.

In 1926 some 61 per cent of the adult population of the states of the Southeast were enrolled in church. This was the largest proportion of any section of the country. The 39 per cent who were not church members were often illiterates, isolated mountaineers, poor whites, and poor Negroes. Among them were persons who might be expected to join the church when they became sufficiently sophisticated to understand the Southern heritage. Or the nonchurch members were persons who inherited a frontier individualism which caused them to abhor the regimentation of church organizations without necessarily abhoring the faith of their British ancestors. They never went to church and were likely to sit on street corners or behind tobacco barns on Sunday morning and tell scandalous tales about the preacher and the female members of his choir. But they would react furiously if a stray interloper attacked the orthodoxies.

Not since 75 years ago when the crackerbox atheist repeated Tom Paine has there been a native in a typical Southern community who shouts unbelief. Today one seldom finds a native of the middle or upper class who has not in some way affiliated with a Christian communion. Never does a Southerner die so depraved in his conduct or so independent in his thinking that he leaves behind him the request that he not be given Christian burial.

If some Southern parents fail to send their children to Sunday School, it is because they are too lazy to get their children fed and dressed in time for the opening activities of the church. Urbanization in the South has not, as elsewhere in Christendom, led to a falling away from God. *The Census of Religious Bodies* demonstrates that church membership in Southern cities has grown more rapidly than whole populations. Between 1916 and 1926, for example, the church membership of Memphis grew 62 per cent and the whole population, 23 per cent; for New Orleans, to cite another typical example, these figures were 35 and 13 per cent, respectively.

The things of Mammon have not caused the Southerner to

put aside the things of God. "Religion," says Bishop Robert Raymond Brown of Arkansas, "grabbed hold of the coat-tail of secular prosperity and growth." The increasing wealth that has enveloped the South in the 1940's and 1950's has not halted the habit of a greater and greater proportion of the section's people to attend church. It may be that prosperity is an important cause of this trend. In the fashion of their Calvinistic ancestors, Southerners are entering God's house to give thanks for the good things of this earth. The new prosperity has made it possible for more people to have automobiles in which to ride to church, to wear the necessary new clothes, and to give funds with which to build church centers. Church buildings have sprung up in the new cities and new suburbs like mushrooms after a summer rain.

The very rich men—the Candlers, the Dukes, the Belks, and the Cannons—have demonstrated their interest in the faith of their fathers by bestowing great sums on church institutions. A Marxian cast of mind might lead one to suspect ulterior motives in these givings. I examined a biography of Methodist Bishop John C. Kilgo, the father-confessor who persuaded James B. Duke to give millions to Methodist causes, to discover whether or not Duke was trying to destroy Methodist prejudices against cigarettes. But after reading this account of Duke's intimate conversations with Kilgo, I discovered that the tobacco capitalist was more interested in making peace with God than in overflowing his pockets with tobacco money.

Not since before the American Revolution has the South attempted to enforce religious conformity by law; it has absolute religious freedom so far as the state is concerned. But it forces religious conformity in a subtle and effective way, irritating the visiting Englishman by asking, "To what church do you belong?" If the answer is "No church whatever," the Southerner turns away bewildered. Unless he is widely read or widely traveled, he can scarcely conceive of a person who is decent in dress, manners, and morals who has no church inclinations.

After 1830 the Southern mind was captured from the Jeffersonian deists and the liberal politicians by a group of orthodox Presbyterian theologians, the most eminent of whom were James H. Thornwell and Robert L. Dabney. These staunch theologians drove the Unitarian Horace Holley from Transylvania University and the deist Thomas Cooper from the South Carolina College. They were as learned in the traditional church lore as the Catholic doctors of the Middle Ages, but they reconciled the teaching of orthodox Protestantism with the conditions of Southern life. They accepted all the local dogmas from the creation of the world by divine fiat to the belief that the Negro got to be like he was because Ham laughed at his drunken father. The secular leaders of the later years of the Old South from Jefferson Davis to Robert E. Lee did not wrestle with doubts as John C. Calhoun and John Randolph of Roanoke wrestled before them; they accepted without question the faith of their learned theologians.

Then, after the Civil War, came "the treason of the clerks." Some of the learned among the clergy abandoned the belief that the Word of God as revealed in the Book provided an unchanging and certain truth before which the demonstrations of scientists and sociologists seemed negligible. Instead they turned to the beliefs of the French *philosophes* and certain advanced American thinkers of the late eighteenth century.

They saw the necessity of reconciling divine truth with the ever-aggressive teachings of science. They would substitute the facts inferred from experiments for the certainties which had been handed down from God to the Prophets and the Apostles.

The issue revolved around a question of fundamental importance: whether man was miraculously made by God in His own image or whether he evolved by natural processes out of lower species as described by Charles Darwin. To orthodox Southerners Darwinism seemed to usurp a principal prerogative of religion by lowering man to the level of animals without the personal moral responsibilities of Christians. The optimistic side of Darwinism, that man was evolving into something better, did not impress those who believed in original sin.

The issue came to a head in 1884 when James Woodrow, of the Columbia Theological Seminary in South Carolina, published his address *Evolution*. This graduate of Heidelberg University maintained that "the Bible does not teach science" and that a sympathetic understanding of the theory of evolution did not lead to doubt but to a more profound reverence for God's plan of creation. The writer of this repudiation of the literal words of the Bible as the unquestioned source of knowledge was accused of teachings calculated to destroy divine authority and was removed from his professorship. But the moral victory was Woodrow's. The bold manner in which he advocated the claims of science on faith was the first step in the spread of unorthodox thinking among the theologians of the South. Thereafter for nearly eighty years the advocates of unyielding orthodoxy were in retreat.

The forces of religious subversion moved ruthlessly for-

ward. Robert L. Dabney, the last of the theological titans out
of the Old South, in lectures and books fought energetically
for three decades against universal education, the industrialization of the South, and such nineteenth century heresies as
evolution, positivism, and pragmatism. He found it convenient to retreat from the Union Theological Seminary in
Virginia to the more orthodox atmosphere of Texas.

The most devastating attack on the old-time faith came
when John T. Scopes, at the behest of individuals largely non-
Southern, flouted at Dayton, Tennessee, the law of Tennessee
forbidding any institution supported by State funds "to teach
the theory that denies the story of divine creation as taught
in the Bible." Scopes and his supporters were the aggressors;
the law-enforcing agencies of Tennessee had made no earlier
attempt to implement the antievolution law in classrooms.

The Dayton courthouse became the scene of a memorable
battle between the orthodox people of the South and those
who demanded academic freedom unhampered by church-
motivated laws. Much to the secret gratification of the evolu-
tionists, Scopes was convicted; the constitutionality of the
antievolution law was upheld by the courts. But the real vic-
tors were Scopes and his friends. The antievolutionary laws
of Tennessee and other Southern states fell into disuse. The
Scopes case was called the Monkey Trial by the press of this
country and of England. The South was ridiculed for allowing such an event to happen.

A most significant fact about the Dayton trial was that
there was no one among the learned theologians of the South
willing to accept the role of prosecutor. That function was assumed by William Jennings Bryan, a conservative in theological matters, hopelessly naïve when confronted with the

complexities of Biblical and scientific interpretations. Clarence
Darrow, the defense attorney, made a fool out of Bryan.

The reality of the matter was that by 1925 a majority of the
high-ranking theological professors of the South and the sophisticated pastors of the big city churches had gone mod-
ernist, or they were too tactful to allow themselves to be convicted of obscurantism in the eyes of the Darwinians of the
North. By that date the most successful—perhaps the most intellectual—members of the clerical profession in the South
were playing down the traditional mission of Christianity,
the saving of souls for the bliss beyond the sky; they were em-
phasizing the social welfare gospel. They were giving advice on everything from how to sleep with a husband or wife
to how to clean up the back streets of the home city. They
were supplementing or supplanting the conventional Southern belief in two heavens, the one beyond the sky and that of
the Old South, by a return to the eighteenth century belief
that, by the invocation of the prescriptions of the sociologists,
something approximating paradise could be attained on this
earth. They thought it was possible to go to heaven without
dying.

Scriptural injunctions such as "My kingdom is not of this
world," "To him that hath shall be given," and "For ye have
the poor with you always," were discounted as cynical aspersions against human improvement. The wisdom of putting
whole trust in a divine dictator was set aside in favor of the
belief in the innate goodness of man. Moral teachings almost
crowded out faith in divinity.

I heard in 1927 a Chicago-educated minister tell students at
a distinguished Methodist institution of learning that it was
more important to live like Jesus than it was to believe in
Jesus. This was ethical culture, a novelty among a people

whose faith flowed from that fountain filled with blood first envisaged in seventeenth century England.

To protest against this type of modernism got one nowhere. To do so brought from the ecclesiastical snobs the charge of being a fool, of catering to the unwashed multitude, or of being ignorant of the discoveries of the Darwinians and the social scientists, with their philosophies of progress and democracy. The laity, in whose hands ultimate authority rests in Southern churches, was not offended by the opinions of highly placed ecclesiastics. Southern laymen were not sophisticated enough to make a distinction between ethics and faith. They assumed that because a clergyman lived in charity with his fellowman, it followed that he also believed in the orthodoxies.

The people of the Confederacy who were literate enough to leave letters and diaries were convinced that the Confederacy could not fail because the Lord God of Battles had raised up such consecrated men as Marse Robert and Stonewall to defend the Southern cause. But the miracle did not happen; the Confederacy did fail. It did so, suggests E. Merton Coulter, the most complete historian of the Confederacy, because Christianity had not yet become a vital interest of the lower masses of Southerners and therefore did not become a much-needed rallying point around which an invincible morale might have been constructed.

Three divines—Bishop Leonidas Polk and the Reverends Mark P. Lowrey and William N. Pendleton—were fighting generals of the Confederacy; the few generals who were not already Christians were converted and baptized; and such powerful divines as James H. Thornwell and Benjamin M. Palmer went among the soldiers fighting sin and urging the

soldiers to slay the Yankees. But during the war scarcely 20
per cent of the civilian and military population was affiliated
with any church.

Even though this 20 per cent has increased to 65 or 70 per
cent since 1865, still there are millions of Southerners of both
races who are ignorant or indifferent to the saving grace of
the Gospel. Many Southerners perhaps have never heard of
Jesus. As revealed by the writings of Erskine Caldwell and
William Faulkner, there is a vast rural underworld of poor
whites and poor Negroes who dance to the beat of juke boxes
Sunday night without knowing about the puritan Sabbath of
other Southerners; they also violate one or more of the Ten
Commandments without having compunctions of conscience.
If there were, as in Colonial Virginia, a law compelling
church attendance, it would do little good among unchurched
Southerners. The poor whites do not have the clothes or the
manners to make them feel at ease in the church; they are
not sophisticated enough to understand the King James Bible
or the "seminary language" of a clergy among whom educational standards are rising.

Yet the failure of the intellectuals among the clergy to adhere to "the old-time religion," and of a large part of the
lower classes to be impressed by the old-time gospel, does not
destroy the claim that the South is one of the most devout
sections of Christendom. The controversies of our intellectuals should not be taken too seriously in an area essentially
rural in its psychology and nonintellectual in its outlook.
Southerners, outside the restricted circles of professors, edi-
tors, and clergymen and other speakers, are hardly aware of
the controversies that have ruffled the feathers of the pundits.
More than a hundred years ago Harriet Martineau, an ob-

servant English traveler, met an English clergyman in Georgia who said that his congregation loved him and looked after his every need, but had not paid enough attention to his sermons to tell him whether they liked them or not. Southerners in the time of Miss Martineau did not listen to sermons. This is still true, if the observations of one who has attended hundreds and even thousands of church services in the South may be taken as valid. My observation is that if a person does not want to be impolite, he had better not after services ask the average worshipper to comment on what the preacher said. If he does so, he will get a shrug of the shoulder or a sharp reply such as, "Why ask me? If you wanted to know what the preacher had to say, why didn't you listen yourself?"

Many of the liberal thinkers of the South in matters of faith have been forced to retreat from their advanced position because their mentors in the theological schools of New York and Chicago in recent years have retreated from their advanced positions. Reinhold Niebuhr, the most eminent of the Northern theologians, has found that "the near moralism of traditional liberalism" of his seminary days has no real answer to the needs of Christian living and Christian thinking. Southern thinkers are slow in catching up with Northern thinkers. But if past performances are a key to future behavior, the Southerners will, before many years, catch up with Niebuhr and other champions of neo-orthodoxy. They will do this or else put themselves in the ridiculous position of imagining themselves "advanced" by holding on to doctrines abandoned in areas intellectually more energetic than the South. Southern liberal theologians are not that foolish. Already they are adopting the new conservatism; already they are growing pessimistic over the hopes of bringing

heaven down to earth; already they are reaffirming the old
dogmas of the church as man's only certain hope. They are
substituting for hopes of progress the expectation of the Second Coming.

Thank
God

The fact that the Southern churches are not democratic
enough to make all sorts and conditions of men comfortable
has certain advantages. This barrier gives the enterprising
among the lower classes something to aspire to: being well
enough dressed, well enough behaved, and well enough in-
formed to give proof that he should become a member of a
church made up of people better off socially and morally than
the class from which he sprang. Whether or not it fits with
American ideals of democracy, climbing the social ladder by
way of the church is as dynamic a force in Southern life as
getting ahead through money, education, or claims to aristocracy. If a Southern church were to become democratic
enough in cultural and social standards to capture that one
fourth of the people who are unchurched, it would be faced
with the peril of perishing for lack of elevating ideals to which
its members could aspire.

The rise of educational standards has reduced illiteracy
among Southerners to a minimum; denominational ideals
are being aspired to by so many members of the lower classes
that before many decades perhaps the number of the unchurched may become as small as the number of illiterates.

The schools of the South have been accused of lowering
their standards to suit the tastes of the meaner elements of
society. The same accusation has been made against the
Primitivist sects that have become so strong in the lower middle classes of the South in the past fifty years. This accusation
is only fair from the viewpoint of rationalists who would re-
duce the emotional and miraculous in Christianity to a mini-

mum. Many trusting souls have been made extremely happy by the acceptance of the belief of the Primitivist churches that faith can do as much for them today as for Christians in the times of the Apostles. Given to prophecy, the Primitivists believe that hidden in the obscurities of the Prophets and the Apocalypse are divinely inspired keys to the future. They are divine healers, believers in heavenly intervention in favor of the sick. They report various experiences with Unknown Tongues and Pillars of Fire, means through which God converses with the Faithful. Frequently they are Premillennialists, believing that Christ would not postpone indefinitely His Second Coming to save His troubled people.

There is nothing in the beliefs of these so-called off-color faiths not accepted by the high-church Episcopalians and other sincere believers in Divine Providence. Southerners of neither race are lured away from the straight and narrow path by such heresies as those of Father Divine. The shouting, screaming, and jumping in which Primitivists indulge is no more irrational than the shouting, screaming, and jumping in which people of high rank indulge at football games; the events narrated in the New Testament are for the Primitivists still the most exciting news the human race ever had.

The greatest misconception of the Bible Belt that Henry L. Mencken and other critics have propagated is that it is preacher-ridden. The weakness of this charge is revealed through the pathetic stories of the ministers in Ellen Glasgow's *Vein of Iron* and William Faulkner's *Light in August*. Southern churches are vestry- or deacon-ridden, with the ministers approaching the role of puppets rather than spiritual dictators. From early Colonial days the South has had a weak church structure, with church installations as a rule modest and the laity in almost absolute control. It is by no means uncommon for love and loyalty to a church by its members to vary in direct proportion to disloyalty, jealousy, and even hatred of the minister. It is not considered entirely improper for respected church members to engage in carping criticisms of their ministers. During the Colonial period the parsons of Virginia were given only one year tenure; today ministers in all Southern states frequently lose their positions because of espousing unpopular causes; witness the large number punished today for opposing the determination of their congregations that the races be kept apart in the house of God.

This lack of independent power by the clergy has obvious disadvantages. It also has its advantages. The effectiveness of lay pressure has kept the great popular churches in harmony with the conservative sentiments of the majority of the Southern people. In the old days the influence of the magnates of the land made the church proslavery and separatist. Today this influence keeps those among the clergy heedful of non-Southern opinion from alienating Southerners from the faith of their fathers. Specifically does it hinder radical experiments in race relations.

The Southern Baptist church is growing faster than any other major denomination in the United States. This is partly because lay control in that church is so complete. Baptist deacons refuse to give up fundamentalist doctrines at the behest of clerical demands that their church unite with the less orthodox Baptist church of the North.

A powerful factor in the growth of certain church bodies in the South is their willingness to adjust themselves to the consistencies of the Southern environment. Some years ago this fact was sympathetically brought to the attention of the

American people by the play *Green Pastures*. This drama may have taken license with prosaic fact by conceiving of God as wearing a frock coat, eating catfish stew, and smoking a fifty-cent cigar. But it is true that in the genuinely popular churches of the two races activities and ceremonials have gone contemporary. The preacher dresses like a businessman and speaks in the vernacular. The choir consists of the prettiest girls in town with rouge on their faces and, until the coming of angel robes, displaying the latest modes. Traditional musical instruments are often supplemented by fiddles and even by trombones; the old-time hymns of a treasured English heritage are often supplemented by tunes that sound like those of the juke boxes.

Attached to the more recent church structures are hotel-like appendages. Even ministers are wont to refer to their church as "the plant." These make possible the development within sacred precincts of activities that would not have been accepted in more austere ages of Protestantism. There everything recreational and even frivolous takes place short of round dancing. There hot dogs in hunks of bread supplement the anemic wafers of the communion table. As Harry Golden wrote in *The Carolina Israelite,* future archeologists may some day excavate the ruins of our civilization and wonder what kinds of sacrifices were offered in the huge bake ovens and barbecue pits discovered in our churches.

This compromise with the contemporary worldly attitudes is what gives the Baptist and Methodist churches advantage in winning the allegiance of the masses as well as the upper class. "The Scotch scotched themselves," says a wise historian. He means that the Presbyterian church declined relatively because it would not fully Americanize itself by dropping to a sufficient degree the customs of Scotland. This is truer still of the Episcopal church where the surplices, prayer books, and formal ritual of an English background are strange to the average Southerner.

Southern churches in ritual and doctrine pursue tactics in important respects opposite to those of Fifth Avenue. The New York churches practice a ritual often as old as the middle ages and a doctrine as modern as Charles Darwin and Thomas Huxley. The Southern churches, except in a few cities and university centers, follow a ritual in harmony with modern American practices and a doctrine as old as that of the seventeenth century. This discriminating application of the new and the old is what gives the Roman Catholic Church strength in such countries as Mexico, Brazil, and Portugal. In those countries the image of the Blessed Virgin satisfies local tastes by being an Indian, a Negress, or a white woman with a double chin.

Once while addressing a Sunday school class I used the example of the confusion of tongues at the Tower of Babel to describe the division of Southern Christians into so many denominations. This repetition by me of an unoriginal assertion already made by a hundred church journalists was contradicted by the wisest member of my audience. "Religion in the South," said this interlocutor, "is like Joseph's garment, a coat of many colors. It is a flawless ensemble." He explained that the battle of the sects so far as the South is concerned is an event of the ante-bellum past. It is no longer good manners, in pulpit or parlor, to criticize a church other than one's own. The different denominations today are cordial toward each other; every Sunday night in summer in some Southern towns they hold union services. A Methodist minister going about the countryside criticizing the Baptists, as did Parson

William G. Brownlow in the 1850's, would today be considered a frightful anomaly. Roman Catholics, though sus-
pected and misunderstood in an overwhelming Protestant
region, have been tolerated since the American Revolution.
The fact that the average rural Southerner is reluctant to vote
for a Catholic is not proof that the Southerner is not willing to
allow the Catholic perfect religious freedom.

This last statement must be qualified. Lord Bryce's assertion that in America there is an unofficial union of church and
state applies with greatest accuracy to the South. Democratic
politicians and old-fashioned liberals were rudely shocked
in 1928 when several Southern states refused to support Al
Smith's candidacy for the presidency largely because he was
a Roman Catholic. Thomas Jefferson's statue in Charlottes-
ville was draped in crepe.

This repudiation of Al Smith was no more than could be
expected by those who appreciate the intense Protestant heritage of the South. Jefferson's admonition to segregate religion and politics in different sides of the head may have
worked well in an age when Jefferson and other members of
the ruling class had little religion to mix with their politics.
It is impossible for the devout Southerner of the twentieth
century not to vote the same way that he prays. He gets concepts of faith, righteousness, and politics so confused that they
could be unraveled only in the unrealistic thinking of those
who think in terms of the geometrical simplicities of the
eighteenth century.

It was inaccurate, though the liberals charged it at the time,
to accuse Southerners of violating religious freedom by voting
as they did in 1928. Few were interested in denying a Roman
Catholic the right to run for office or the right to worship
God as he pleased. Moreover, it is feasible to believe that

Southerners voted against Al Smith because of the political rather than the doctrinal implications of Catholicism. They have often been willing to vote for high-church Episcopalians who are doctrinally akin to Catholics, but who, unlike Catholics, do not owe allegiance to a foreign potentate. A Catholic candidate for President in 1960 was successful in many Southern states because he pledged Southern clergymen that he adhered rigidly to the doctrine of the separation of church and state.

The South today holds to denominational differences to a greater degree than it did in the frontier days when because of inadequate housing different denominations shared the same church buildings. The Community or United Church Movement of the North and of Canada has made little progress in the South because of social reasons and because a pious people interpret narrowly the teachings of Jesus.

Southerners adhere firmly to the Christian dogma that there is but a single road by which a person can be saved. Because each denomination believes that it has the right road to the Heavenly Kingdom, there is no room for compromise with those who claim other roads. The devout Southerner thinks that to meet other Christians on common grounds of belief might leave only a residue of vague affirmations closely kin to Unitarianism or Universalism. His dogmas are too exclusive for that. It might also create something beyond his understanding, a religion that is not a religion, an ethical culture that has not thrived in the South since the time of Jefferson. The Southerner believes that it is hardly possible to lead an exemplary life unless that life stems from faith in the Resurrected Lord. The thought has never entered his mind in the past one hundred and fifty years that it is possible to follow Christ's teachings without a precise affirmation of His divinity such as given in the creeds of the different denominations.

Despite loud denials by the official keepers of the Southern conscience, the region below the Potomac accepts strong social distinctions. Its proclamations of democracy so far as group relations are concerned are largely a pose. It therefore follows that the churches, in order to accommodate themselves to the regional realities, must accept these social distinctions with grace. In fact there is no conscious problem of adjusting the all sorts and conditions of men to the separate religious denominations that conform to their several humors and dispositions. Everyone is satisfied with these divisions; he seeks naturally in church, as in other aspects of social relations, his own level.

The Southerner of all classes has never been willing to kowtow to his betters. He therefore does not want to be thrown in church with those who do not wish to associate with him in a free and easy fashion. The propaganda for social democracy in which all churches indulge is no fit substitute, in the thinking of the proud Southerner, for the informal comradeship he is able to give and get from members of his own class. So, without formal decree to that effect, certain social types become members of the Episcopal church; other types join the Presbyterian, Methodist, Baptist, and Primitivist church bodies. What are the social distinctions that bring about these denominational differences is hard to say, but everyone who knows the South knows that these differences exist.

These separations are not only interdenominational but exist within the denominations. In the typical Virginia town in which I live are three Methodist churches. One is for Negroes; another is dominated by the artisan and laboring

classes among the whites; a third is dominated by the professional and merchant classes. These church divisions along social lines just happened without any thought on the part of
anyone that they were not meet and right.

That the separation of the churches along social lines is as
immutable as the procession of the seasons is illustrated by
what happened in the little town in South Carolina in which
I was born. It had three Baptist churches—one for Negroes,
another for the white cotton mill operatives, and a third for
those who were prosperous or given to aristocratic conceits.
Our ambitious politician—one who now holds high office—
had learned in his sociology classes at college that social distinction (within the white race) before the throne of God
should be abolished. He implemented his belief by having the
church in the mill village discontinued in hope that all white
Baptists could worship in the same sanctuary. This attempted
revolution proved abortive. The more modest among the
mill operatives organized a Holy Roller church, and when
the bolder spirits out of the destroyed church entered the
church of the prosperous and the family-conscious, many of
the snobs in the latter church—those who had been to college
and had learned to drink cocktails, or belonged to the highest
ranking families—withdrew from the church of their ancestors and joined the Episcopal church.

The segregation of races in the churches often provokes
bitter attacks on Southern denominations. Condemnatory res-
olutions are passed by assemblies of churchmen both within
and without the South. The separation of the races in church
is said to be a mockery of the Christian ideal of the Father-
hood of God and the Brotherhood of Man. The exclusion of
the colored race from the white's man's house of God is as
rigid as in any other aspects of the color line. Today—except

in the case of deliberate experiments carried on by a few progressive clergymen—a visitor never sees a Negro in a white
church. It would take more courage than most Negroes have
for one to crash the gates.

It was not thus in slavery days, and I can remember almost
a half century ago in my home church in South Carolina
half the congregation was composed of Negroes. They sat
in the back of the sanctuary and took the Holy Communion
after the whites; but after the acts of worship they lingered
in the church yard to participate in the small talk with the
white parishioners.

I regret that this type of interracial familiarity has van-
ished. If I were to tell the younger members of my old congregation that our church once had a large Negro membership they would suspect me of playing on my imagination.

The separation of the races in church started with the abolition of slavery. A little historical investigation will prove that
it was more on the initiative of the Negro than the white
man. The whites were reluctant to surrender the rigid control they had over their Negro members under slavery. The
Negroes, on the other hand, felt that their accustomed habit
of religious subordination to the master race was incompatible
with their status as freedmen. They demanded the elementary American constitutional right of religious freedom, including separate church organizations and congregations,
and ministers and church officials of their own race and
choosing.

Realizing the separation was inevitable, the whites of most
denominations allowed the blacks to withdraw in peace, often
helping them financially in the building of separate churches.
Typical of what happened is the experience of the First Baptist Church at Montgomery, which came out of the Civil War

with three hundred white members and six hundred colored members. When it was felt wise to separate, the two races co-operated in the erection of a new church for the Negro members, who continued to use the old church while theirs was being built. When all was ready, the colored congregation was launched with the blessings of the whites. The whites of Montgomery, as elsewhere in the South, were confident that structural independence would not be accompanied by doctrinal innovations abhorrent to Southern tradition. It is a tribute to Christian tolerance that this parting of the ways took place without the acrimony that characterized the political estrangements of the Reconstruction period. The South fortunately has no heritage of racial hatred along religious lines.

The largest number of blacks joined the Negro Baptist church where they were allowed the maximum independence from white control. The white Baptists were prompter than other denominations in granting the Negroes church autonomy. They facilitated the ordination of Negro ministers by not demanding as high educational standards as Presbyterians and Episcopalians. Soon the white Baptists learned to be almost indifferent to the religious behaviour of the blacks; this made it possible for Negro Baptists to do as they pleased.

The Methodists lost heavily in their Negro membership because, in the crucial years immediately after the war, they did not grant the blacks the right to have independent congregations. Because the Episcopal church has down to the present failed to give its Negroes an independent church organization, it has lost almost all of its colored members, except a few among the elite. Negro Episcopalians are forced to submit to the authority of a white episcopate.

"Does Dr. Addleman love you?" I asked a Negro professor of a Negro college of the college's sponsoring bishop. "Yes, he does," was the reply; "he has spent much time and energy collecting money among the white people to make our college prosperous." I then asked the Negro professor, "Do you love Dr. Addleman?" The reluctant reply was, "I ought to love him but I don't. He has done so much for us. But he demands and receives more kowtowing from his Negro beneficiaries than he could ever get from white persons. Unconsciously this Southern gentleman is a snob."

Then my informer, as a member of a race that understands the white man better than the white man understands the Negro, made this generalization. "The white man in the United States, whether he is a liberal or a conservative, a Democrat, a Republican, or a Communist, demands the right to dominate in social relations with Negroes. This is especially true when the white man has benevolent intentions. Most of us Negroes have the privilege of avoiding contacts with whites in our church relations, and we intend to exercise this privilege even to the extent of depriving ourselves of gifts that might come our way."

The right to have an independent church is the greatest liberty the Negro won as the result of his Reconstruction experience. It is a privilege all white Southerners, with the exception of a few philanthropists, are willing for him to have. The white man's respect for religion gives the Negro church a freedom from intrusion that is not enjoyed in other aspects of Negro life. The Negro church, says Gunnar Myrdal, the most complete student of American race relations, "is such a good community center that it might almost be said that anyone who does not belong to the church in the rural South does not belong to the community." As Richard Wright, the Negro novelist, puts it, "Our churches are where we dip our

tired bodies in cool springs of hope, where we retain our
wholeness and humanity despite the blow of death from the
Bosses. . . ."

The same could be said of Southerners in the middle of the
twentieth century that Richard M. Weaver said of them when
they embarked on the Civil War: they were "one of the few
religious people left in the Western World." The conversion
of some of the clergy of the recent South to modernism is
counterbalanced by a much larger proportion of the Southern
people in the Christian fold at present than in ante-bellum
days. The masses of both races are feeling with greater intensity than ever before the influence of the Christian affirmations. Those who twenty-five years ago were compromising
before the secular and materialistic influences that came from
the North are now being influenced by the neo-orthodoxy
coming from Europe and the North. There is today a Solid
South based on faith more uniting than the Solid South based
on politics. The Holy Rollers and the members of the upper
class churches are divided more by social distinctions than
by distinctions of doctrines. Both are dominated by natural
piety and hostility to rationalism and free inquiry in Biblical
matters. Conservatism in faith did not rank far behind racial
attitudes as a significant cause of the South's retention of its
regional distinctiveness.

Much criticism is still hurled at the South because of its
peculiar customs. In politics, in social relations, and in schools
its racial attitudes have been challenged in Congress and by
the Supreme Court because of their supposed violation of re-
strictions imposed on the States by the United States Constitution. Time alone will tell how effective these challenges
will be. But the Constitution proclaims absolute religious

freedom and gives no pretext for outside interference in the ways Southerners conduct their churches. The region therefore bids fair to retain indefinitely its freedom of action in this field, and through the dynamic influence of religion maintain the regional identity.